S0-BFD-214

Paid for from:
ATOD Prevention Program Funds
Eau Claire Area School District
500 Main Street
Eau Claire, WI 54701

CREATING THE CONDITIONS
LEADERSHIP FOR QUALITY SCHOOLS

DIANE GOSSEN & JUDY ANDERSON

Cover Design by Paul Turley

Text Layout by Douglas Gibson & Dixon Smith

ISBN 0-944337-26-0

Library of Congress Catalog Card Number: 95-067529

Quantity Purchases

Companies, professional groups, clubs and other organizations may
qualify for special terms when ordering quantities of this title. For
ordering information contact the Sales Department, New View Publications, P. O. Box 3021, Chapel Hill, NC 27515-3021.

1-800-441-3604

The character on the preceding page means encounter, a meeting of
minds and experiences. It is more than physically meeting someone: the
character has the connotation of getting to know deeper, of establishing
a relationship, of developing an intuitive understanding of a person. This
book is the two authors' insights and suggestions which come from
knowing intuitively and relating, over time.

To the Sheridan Hills staff, students, and parents, with whom we journeyed on our quest for quality.

CONTENTS

ACKNOWLEDGMENTS

We would like first and foremost to recognize Dr. William Glasser as our teacher and mentor. We are both grateful that in 1965 he decided to take the ideas of reality therapy into the educational community. He has never looked back and has inspired many of us around him with his vision. His willingness to devote two weeks to reviewing this book in depth and suggesting revisions challenged us to greater quality.

Both of us honor the Johnson City School District and the work of John Champlin, Al Mamary, Larry Rowe and Frank Alessi. They went before us in district-wide Quality School change and we commend them for their courage, as well as thank them for their teaching.

There are several school districts that were willing to dialogue with us and experiment with our ideas as we developed them—Richfield School District in Minneapolis, Minnesota; Evergreen School District in Washington state; Quesnel School District in British Columbia, Canada; Tumwater School District in Washington state; and the Truckee Elementary School in California. Each of the districts committed to train all of their people in the Quality

School model, and we feel they were our teachers in our adventure.

Diane would like to thank Innovation Associates, Peter Senge's organization, for teaching her their systems model, and Tom Zenisek for teaching her about homeorhesis. For three summers she also had the privilege of working with the Control Systems Group. The opportunity to listen to William Powers as he dialogued with us about Control Theory across the disciplines of physics, biology, education, economics, medicine, theology, computers, and music was a peak experience to be treasured.

Although there are many individual schools with whom we have worked, we have dedicated our book to Sheridan Hills, Judy's school. Also, both of us have benefited from teaching with our colleagues in the Quality School movement.

We particularly appreciate the support of Perry and Fred Good of New View Publications for their faith in our work. We thank Rosita and Genevieve Tam for their contributions. The artful Chinese characters and descriptions they provided for us add another level of meaning to our book.

We are grateful we had three teenagers with whom to practice: Judy's Nate and Nora, and Diane's Jake. They taught us a lot about loving negotiations.

There are two people without whom this book would not exist. Sara Davis, our editor, was creative and scrupulous in her careful work to pull together our disparate efforts. Jackie Eaton, Diane's executive assistant, led us all by modelling problem solving, collaboration and non-critical support for all who worked on this book.

FOREWORD

What a Quality School is, is described in my book, *The Quality School*. What a teacher is advised to do to create a quality classroom in a Quality School is described in my book, *The Quality School Teacher*. What I do not describe is the process for getting there, the process for changing from a boss-managed or fear system to a lead-managed or support system. I did not do this because I do not lead a school: only a principal aided by someone like myself could do this. Judy Anderson is such a principal. Diane Gossen, who has worked with me in schools since 1968, is someone who is experienced with the ideas we have taught and used for years. In this book, they have joined to tell all who are interested how to create the conditions that will make it possible for a school to move to a Quality School. Read my books carefully, then put what is in this book into practice and you are on your way.

William Glasser, M.D.

PREFACE

We have been involved in the Quality School movement for several years, Diane as a Quality School consultant and Judy as a school principal. Our collaboration began in 1992 when Judy's district began studying the Quality School ideas. The process that we experienced was not quick and easy. It required a personal change, a systems change, and a major shift in thinking.

As we began to work with other school leaders interested in Quality School ideas, we encountered the same questions from everyone: How do we get started? How is a Quality School different from our school? What are the dynamics of the change process? How long will it take to become a Quality School? We began to talk with leaders in the Quality School movement to discover how they were addressing these questions. In our conversations and through our experience, we discovered that there is no **right** way to implement the Quality School: it is not a sequential process. Yet each journey to quality shared the similar changes in direction: from an external to an internal locus of control; from a stimulus-response to a control theory view of the world; from positive reinforcement to self-evaluation; from good work to quality work; from boss management to lead management; from coercion to consensus and collaboration.

This book will lead you through our experience with certain models that we have used to implement the Quality School. They comprise the psychological basis of control theory, the Quality School model of William Glasser, M.D., the Systems Change Model of the Johnson City School District, and the Fourteen Points of Quality of W.E. Deming. You will have the opportunity to use specific experiential learning activities that show what to expect during the change process. We have also combined the work of many others who have written about personal change, systems change, group process strategies, personal renewal, and lead management.

The purpose of this book is to answer the five most commonly asked questions by those who are interested in becoming a Quality School:

1. How do we begin?

2. What is the process?

3. What strategies are useful?

4. What will we look like?

5. What kind of school and what kind of people do we want to be?

These questions are often difficult to answer. In fact, our experience has been that many schools spend a couple of years seriously examining them. The answer to the first two questions involves gaining new knowledge about Quality School ideas, internalizing control theory, learning group process skills and creating a shared vision. These stages of the change process are exciting because people enjoy learning new ideas and skills.

By the third year, however, people begin to ask, "Is what we are now doing aligned with our new knowledge and our shared vision?" Some may be personally threatened. They may say, "Let's think about this a while longer. We need more information. Maybe this isn't what we want. Is what we are doing aligned with what we know, want, and believe?" The answer to these questions mark the commencement of change, but they also may result in the end of the move towards quality. People may become worried about changing practices and the changing system. Personal change happens before systems change, and systems change takes place before aligning practices. All three are critical components of becoming a Quality School.

In the fourth year, a school's successes begin to be noticed by others. Visitors come to see what everyone is talking about. At this stage it is important to stay focused on the shared vision, rather than on what the visitors *believe* the school has become. Schools can get caught up in a stimulus-response mode and stop progressing because they are influenced by the positive attention from others. In order to avoid this, the staff in a Quality School asks themselves, "What do we want to become?"

We named this book *Creating the Conditions* because the role of the quality leader is to *create the conditions* that promote cooperation, creativity, quality work and self-evaluation. Once these conditions are in place, it is the responsibility of the staff to choose whether or not to integrate these concepts into their personal and professional lives. When staff begin to ask themselves, "If I continue to do what I am doing now, what are my chances of getting what I want?" real change in behavior, on a personal or organizational level, can take place. If change does not occur, then the leader's role is to self-evaluate, asking "Even though the change has not come about, have I been the leader I want to be? Have I been caring and courageous? Have I taken responsibility when I can?"

We wrote *Creating the Conditions* especially for school principals, site-based team members, core team members, and other school administrators who are looking for ways to get to the answers. Yet, this book could also help teachers relate more effectively with their students, parents, and colleagues. Part One, Getting Started, deals with cognitive and personal change. Moving Forward provides information regarding systems change and will help you answer the second question, "What is the process?" Getting Unstuck deals with culture change and helps staff learn to resolve conflicts through collaboration. Aligning Practices focuses on program change and discusses group process strategies that will help answer the question, "What will we look like?" The chapter on Continuous Renewal contemplates the future of the Quality School by focusing on the question, "What do we want to become?"

Throughout the book, we have used the word "leader" instead of "manager," and the phrase "quality leader" rather than "lead-manager." We are going to speak with you as if we were working with you and your staff. Please feel free to receive what we say just as information and take only what fits for you at this time. It is our sincere hope that this book will provide you with information and skills that will help you on your journey to becoming a Quality School.

Diane Gossen and Judy Anderson

GETTING STARTED

Look within and you will find who you can become. The character on the preceding page represents illumination, energy, power and stability. All of these are the result of looking within and initiating growth and change. This chapter gives ways to look within. Control theory helps us to see our ideal pictures and understand our behaviors.

GETTING STARTED

Dr. William Glasser's book *The Quality School* (New York: Harper and Row, 1990) has been in the hands of educators for five years. "Managing Students without Coercion" is the subtitle of the book, but managing without coercion is not easy. Schools moving towards Quality experience both triumphs and trials.

After teachers read the book, many are excited. They begin to think of ways to reduce fear and coercion, emphasize quality work, and invite self-evaluation. Many teachers report with enthusiasm their success with even difficult students. They follow Dr. Glasser's advice and start small. Some teachers replace classroom rules with classroom agreements. Some schools post throughout the school, "At our school we solve problems with nobody getting hurt." Instead of telling students, "Do this or we'll hurt you," they say, "Do this and it will bring quality to your life." These changes work at first. Initially the enthusiasm of teachers and students support the new ideas, but soon the newness wears off and the hard work of becoming a Quality School begins.

DEVELOPMENTAL STAGES OF THE CHANGE PROCESS

Going from enthusiasm to despair is a normal part of most significant change. Realizing that change is developmental and a process, not an event, can help you create the conditions for staff to satisfy their needs at each stage. We have organized the chapters of this book around these stages of the implementation process: cognitive change, personal change, systems change, culture change, program change, and continual change.

Cognitive Change (Information)

New information frequently initiates a desire for change because people begin to receive new pictures as to how things might be. If others have done it, it can be done! Sometimes best knowledge is in the form of research. Other times it is shared experience from others. Sometimes new information comes as a direct, immediate observation of a new phenomenon which we perceive. New information in the Quality School movement comes from Dr. Glasser's book, *The Quality School*, from videotapes, workshops, site visits, and dialogues with others. The important question at this time is, "Do I understand?"

Personal Change (Building New Pictures)

As we examine new information, we begin the process of personal change. Personal change results when we compare new perceptions coming in with previous pictures we hold as how things should be. Each person needs to reflect, sift, analyze, and choose how to perceive this new information. It is also at this point that decisions are made as to whether or not the new information fits with what is known. "If others can do it, so can I...but do I want to do it?" Dialogue and personal reflection are the main vehicles for change at this point. Learning control theory at this point will greatly assist staff. As people learn that they have basic needs and that they have different pictures as to how they meet their needs, they can decide how to perceive situations. The key question here is, "Do I want to experiment with these ideas?"

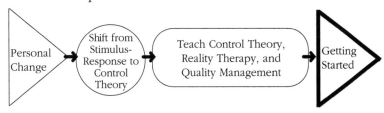

Personal Change → Shift from Stimulus-Response to Control Theory → Teach Control Theory, Reality Therapy, and Quality Management → Getting Started

Systems Change (Management)

In a quality school, the focus from the start and throughout is on changing the system. This is because stimulus-response, boss-managed systems do not work for the challenge of the 21st century. Therefore, instead of trying to fix a bad system, the focus of this book is on changing the system to what Dr. Glasser described in *The Quality School*, and detailed further in *The Quality School*

Teacher. A quality school cannot come into existence unless it is based on a need-satisfying environment.

A major mission of a quality school is to eliminate both discipline problems and the labeling of students as learning disabled through the use of a new system. Any real change for the better in dealing with discipline comes from this systemic change. Many people working in schools today believe the system is right and it is the students that need to change. However, the quality school belief—that the system needs to change, not the student—is consistent with the teaching of W.E. Deming that ninety-four percent of the problem is with the system, not the people.

The main job for a quality leader trying to create new conditions is to change the system. There is always a great deal of pressure to stay with an old, traditional system and try to make it a bit better. It is hard to take a stand on the need to change the system, but Dr. Glasser says the only hope for eliminating both discipline problems and learning disabilities is to change the system, and the core of this systemic change is managing staff and students without coercion. Instead of thinking of the system as something "out there," people with a Control theory perspective realize the system is "within" themselves. Quality leaders invite people to share their personal visions of what they want to be. They understand the most important resource in the system is the people. If the people within a system change, then the system changes.

Systems change is based on personal change. As people decide to embrace new information, they need to decide how to work together in a different way based on their new understanding. Seeking to understand from different perspectives will help each person to sort how and where to stand on an issue. Holding several perspectives in the mind at one time creates the conditions for a paradigm shift. "If others can do it so can we, but how?" At this juncture staff need to be given process-centered tools for visioning, consensus-building and making social contracts. The main question is, "Do we know what we want to be together?"

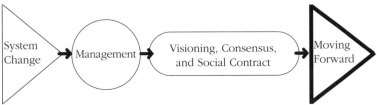

System Change → Management → Visioning, Consensus, and Social Contract → Moving Forward

Culture Change (Conflict Resolution)

Culture change occurs when people change the system based on their new information and perspectives. Culture change is based on action. It is where "the rubber hits the road." Decisions have to be made and there is always conflict, "If others do it, we can do it. We want to do it and we know how to do it but we're getting stuck." When people find themselves stuck, it's time to learn conflict-resolution skills. The culture will shift away from coercive interactions only when people learn to use control theory for win/win solutions. The main question here is, "Do we know how to do this without people getting hurt?"

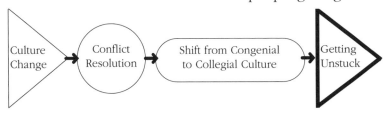

Culture Change → Conflict Resolution → Shift from Congenial to Collegial Culture → Getting Unstuck

Program Change (Alignment)

Program change is based on group decisions which are seated in win/win practices. The alignment of what we want with what we believe based on best knowledge to evaluate what we are doing is the key. The success connection questions based on reality therapy are used here. "If we want to do it and we know why we want to do it and we know how to do it without anyone losing, let's do it!" Some program changes that we have seen have been changes in reading programs, changes to multi-age class groupings, changes from the discipline of consequences to a variety of reality therapy techniques, including self-evaluation and restitution, changes from central budgeting to site-based budgeting and hiring, changes from emphasizing tests and grades to alternate assessments and portfolios. The main question to ask at this stage is, "Is doing this getting us what we want?"

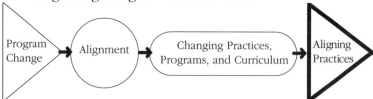

Continual Change (Renewal)

Renewal is based on all the previous changes. If we change ourselves personally can we change the system? If we change the system can we manage the change? If we manage the change are we finished? Hardly! It has been said that the only constant is change. Why is this? Control theory would say it's because we are continually resetting our expectations to get more quality. Change theory would tell us that any time a part changes the whole of which we are a part changes. The important question at this point is "Do we have systems in place for continual self-evaluation and renewal?"

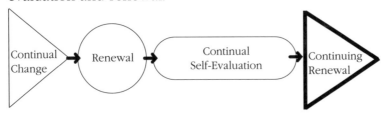

The chart on the next page outlines the chapters of the book in relationship to the stages of the implementation process, and also includes the focus of each chapter. These stages correspond to the Concerns-Based Adoption Model (CBAM) developed by Gene Hall. This model outlines seven stages of concern that people go through in the implementation of any new program or innovation (see appendix). The most important message of CBAM is to direct attention to the needs of the people who will change. This model is consistent with control theory because it focuses on creating a needs-satisfying environment as people go through the stages of concern.

Figure 1. **Implementation Model**

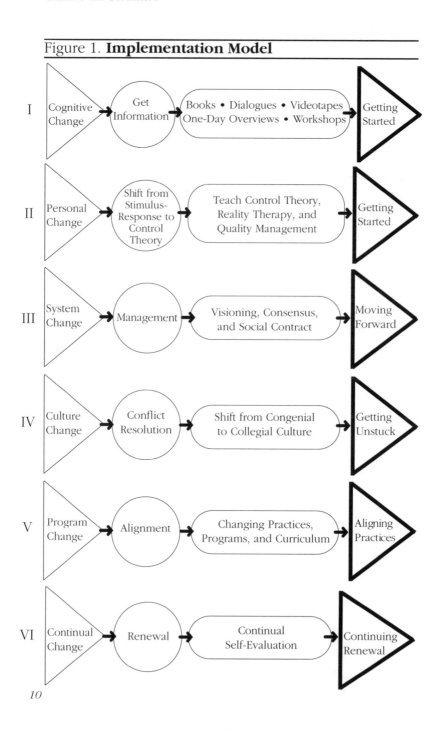

COGNITIVE CHANGE

The question we are asked most frequently is, "How do we get started?" The goal as you get started is to create the conditions under which people will enroll themselves in the learning organization. There are many ways to move toward this goal.

One way to move toward this goal is to talk with the staff about the knowledge-driven learning organization and what being such an organization means. In *The Fifth Discipline* (New York: Doubleday, 1990), Peter Senge writes, "Learning in organizations means the continuous testing of experience, and the transformation of that experience into knowledge—accessible to the whole organization, and relevant to its core purpose." This transformation of experience is accomplished by asking the three reality therapy questions: "What do we want?" "What are we doing to get what we want?" and "Is it working?" When the answer is, "What we are doing is not getting us what we want," the quality leader seeks more information and provides abundant opportunities for the staff to gain information as well.

People are looking for quick fixes or recipes, but there aren't any. In *The Fifth Discipline*, Senge suggests three guidelines for leaders working to create the conditions for enrollment: enroll yourself, be on the level, and let the other person choose. He says that "the hardest lesson for many leaders to face is that, ultimately, there is nothing you can do to get another person to enroll or commit. Enrollment and commitment require freedom of choice."

Leaders are only responsible for fostering a climate of cooperation, creativity, and quality work. They are not responsible if the people in the organization do not take advantage of this climate. This is an important distinction for leaders to make, especially when they self-evaluate. A leader needs to determine whether optimum conditions are established, then ask: "Even though the desired change has not occurred, have I been the leader I want to be? Have I been both caring and courageous? Have I done everything I can do?" When leaders make this distinction, they free themselves from feeling responsible for the outcome. As a result, leaders are less likely to resort to persuasion, they are less invested in their staff's performance, and the conditions are created for the staff to self-evaluate.

In the initial stages of introducing most new ideas or programs, people are usually open to learning, and this has been our experience as we have introduced the ideas of the Quality School. However, people have different learning styles, so it is important to provide a variety of ways for them to learn. One way of introducing staff to these ideas is to invite a reality therapy faculty member to make a presentation on the Quality School. In addition, staff members might attend a Quality School conference, such as the Quality School Consortium Conference (held in October) and the Partners for Quality Learning Conference (usually held in November in Phoenix, Arizona).

Another way of introducing Quality School concepts is to provide multi-media materials. In the bibliography we have listed some excellent resources. The staff-development materials that accompany these videotape series include involvement activities to help staff engage in meaningful dialogue to begin internalizing these powerful ideas.

In fact, dialogue is another good way to educate staff about Quality School concepts. One springboard to dialogue is to buy staff members their own personal copies of books such as *The Quality School, In Pursuit of Happiness,* and *Restitution.* Teachers appreciate having their own books because it helps if they can highlight sections and write notes in the margins. But instead of requiring teachers to read, invite them to learn more about Quality Schools and assess whether the ideas have meaning for them.

The senior quality leader in the organization may then initiate a philosophy circle with staff about the books they are reading. Ron Patterson, the Deputy Director General of the Protestant School Board of Greater Montreal, engaged in dialogue with administrators for an entire year before initiating change. He believes these Thursday lunch discussions laid the groundwork for the shift to the Quality School paradigm. Jean Suffield, Assistant Director General of the South Shore School District, also initiated such discussions when she realized her district was moving to implementation without engaging in enough dialogue and reflection.

Resistant staff may become involved in these groups if they are personally invited, and they can make significant contributions to the school's ability to self-evaluate. Once staff have engaged in dialogue about the Quality School concepts and have made a commitment to move towards quality, the next phase involves training in reality therapy and control theory. Some schools sign a contract to join the Quality School Consortium, which includes intensive weeks of training in these two key concepts, as outlined by Dr. Glasser in *The Quality School.* Several other

Quality School training programs exist, including Partners for Quality Learning, which contracts with individual school districts to implement the Quality District. In these districts the expectation is that all staff will be continuous learners in control theory.

Schools that have participated in both Quality School and Quality District training programs debate about which change should come first—the systems change or the personal change. Some ask if they can be introduced simultaneously. We believe districts and schools can self-evaluate and answer this questions for themselves.

As authors, however, we have decided to focus first on personal change because of our own training experience with schools. Knowing that different people have different pictures and that this is normal helps to set an environment for creating common beliefs and expectations. We have heard many teachers and administrators say that they wish that they had understood control theory before they began the systems change.

CONTROL THEORY

Control theory is the psychological foundation for the Quality School. Experts in the field of organizational management, including Deming and Senge, have acknowledged the supremacy of internal motivation in the search for quality, and they have advocated the necessity of systems that permit satisfaction of individuals' needs. Control theory, developed by Dr. William Glasser, based on the work of William Powers is the theory that explains this psychology. We assume you already have a basic understanding of control theory, or that you will be going in that direction, through some of the means previously described.

PARADIGM SHIFT TO CONTROL THEORY

Control theory is the basis for personal change in the learning organization, but understanding control theory requires a significant change in thinking. One of the challenges of becoming a Quality School leader or building a quality organization is that making this change invites us to examine our basic beliefs. Dr. Glasser says:

> The number-one priority of the administrators in a Quality School is how can we encourage, help and support our teachers both professionally and personally to try out new ideas.
>
> The Quality School, *p. 184*

We all operate on "mental models" which are our quality world pictures that help us understand the world and how we take action. Each of our assumptions, no matter how firmly held, is open to challenge at the intellectual level and at the level of one's experience. However, we often operate unaware of our mental models or the effects they have on our behavior. If we remain unaware of our mental models, the models remain unexamined and therefore unchanged.

In managing mental models at the personal level, Peter Senge talks in *The Fifth Discipline* about the importance of "asking yourself what you believe about the way the world works." Then ask yourself, *Am I willing to consider that this generalization may be inaccurate or misleading?* It is important to ask the second question because if the answer is no, there is no point in proceeding. Even if the answer is yes, Senge recognizes that the "inertia of deeply entrenched mental models can overwhelm even the best systemic insights" (pp. 177-178).

As quality leaders we look inward and find our pictures of what we believe. Each of us examines our own leadership practices. Do we harbor the illusion that we can make others conform? Do we believe it is our responsibility to coerce? Or do we accept that each individual has the right to free choice providing he does not interfere with others meeting their needs?

Quality leaders remember that each of our assumptions represents a mental model that is strongly held in our culture. For example, the stimulus-response mental model we were taught tells us that other people can make us happy or angry or sad, and that our behavior is a response to their actions. Our management methods are then based on finding ways to control others so they do not control us. There are treatises written on techniques of motivation and reinforcement in the belief that these tactics improve performance. Quality leaders may find it difficult to move from their belief in external motivation to an approach which focuses on intrinsic motivation.

Consider the question: How does one make a shift from a stimulus-response perspective to a control theory approach? Some may think this shift in perspective happens through slow, incremental changes in attitude or behavior, but it does not work that way. Stephen R. Covey, in *Principle-Centered Leadership* (New York: Summit Books, 1990) warns that "if you want to make slow, incremental improvement, change your attitude or behavior" (p. 173). On the other hand, he emphasizes that if you want to improve in major ways, you change your frame of reference. "Change how you see the world, how you think about people...Change your paradigm, your scheme for understanding and explaining certain aspects of reality."

Control theory postulates that people do not behave in response to external stimuli, but rather are internally motivated. Control theory turns our thinking about the world upside down.

Figure 2. **Competing Views of the World**	
Stimulus-Response View	**Control Theory View**
Our realities are the same.	Our realities are separate.
Everybody sees the same pictures.	Everybody has different pictures.
We try to convert people to our view of the world.	We try to understand the other person's view of the world.
Misbehavior is seen as a mistake.	All behavior is seen as purposeful.
I can control others.	I can't control others.
Others can control me.	One can only control oneself.
Coercion is practiced when persuasion fails.	Collaboration and consensus create new options.
Limited resources.	Unlimited resources.
Minimum degrees of freedom.	Maximum degrees of freedom.
Win/lose mental model.	Win/win mental model.

With this summary in mind, let us take a closer look at how control theory supports personal change in the learning organization.

INTERNAL MOTIVATION

Control theory identifies four basic psychological needs encoded in our genetic instructions: love, power, fun, and freedom, as well as the physical need for survival. We are born with internal directives, and we behave throughout our lifetimes, to satisfy these needs through whatever means we have learned or can create.

Each of us is going into the world each day attempting to meet our needs for love, power, freedom, and fun, and to survive. Our paths cross and we bump into each other and we irritate each other. Sometimes we do so in a calculated manner, but more often we do it unaware of the consequences, unaware of the other's intent, and unaware of how our actions affect others.

Pictures and Perceptions

Each of us looks out into the world each morning and creates our individual reality. We may see, hear, taste, smell, and touch the same things in the world, but we experience them differently depending on our sensory acuity, our previous experiences in the world, and the level of perception at which we choose to process incoming data. It is amazing indeed that we are able to communicate with each other and furthermore to establish common goals.

The miracle is that we can talk together at all about anything...So how do we ever come to believe that the meaning you get is the one I intended? Very often it's not the same. We only think it's the same, and sometimes fatally, assume it's the same. Finding out if it *is* the same is basically impossible, but even reaching some level of confidence in the sameness requires a long process of back-and-forthing, of cross checking.

William Powers, Living Control Systems, Volume I, *1989, p.286*

Pictures

Pictures refers to our uniquely personal and very specific ideas about what will meet our needs, what we want. It is the concept that explains the above observation about the marvel of communication. It is complex because we can only guess at another person's picture of a want. If we ask them to describe what they want, we can get closer, but even then there can be confusion.

Try ordering rare meat in a restaurant. What is your picture of rare meat? We have been served everything from the faintest hint of pink to meat that was not cooked at all except seared on the outside. How do you order your picture of meat? Since rare is in our picture album, we have tried observing the context. What kind of restaurant is it? Based on our experience of upscale, rare will probably mean blue or close to raw. In that case, medium rare would be our order. If it is a diner, rare could well mean well done, in which case we would refuse it. We personally have resorted to describing a continuum: "Rare but not uncooked, pink but still soft, wet but not on the hoof."

Another example of confusion from different pictures comes from Diane's experience teaching control theory and reality therapy in the prison system. The courses were immediately embraced by the most punitive staff because their picture of control was not self-control but rather excessive force over others. Their picture of reality therapy was translated into giving the inmate a verbal shove with the comment, "Face it, baby, that's reality." Each of these was in direct contradiction to Diane's picture and to the principles of reality therapy and control theory.

Individuals' pictures are unique, and each individual has a unique collection. We sometimes refer to this as a "picture album." Everybody builds a unique collection of pictures derived from life experiences of need-satisfaction. This picture album, also called the "quality world," represents all the specific, detailed wants used as a standard for evaluating perceptions of the real world.

Perceptions

There are two filters between the real world and our ideal world—the knowledge filter and the valuing filter. Through these filters passes information which we initially have received through our senses. In the first filter, the knowledge filter, we organize our experience of the world. We identify sensation—hot, cold, hard, soft, etc.—and configuration. Having recognized its form, we know how to use what we experience.

In the second filter, the valuing filter, we decide whether the use which we recognize is good or bad, depending on the context and on what we believe. Some of you may have seen a hot-chocolate frother from Mexico. To see it, each of you would recognize it as hard, made of wood, etched with decoration in black. You could hypothesize its use, but unless you have knowledge of it, you may guess it is a musical instrument or a child's rattle, and you have no idea of its function because you don't recognize it. Because of this, you can't evaluate this tool as positive or negative. Someone could designate it as an instrument of torture. If you accept this knowledge, you would value the hot-chocolate frother as negative.

Cross-cultural examples of perceptual difference are always fun to process. Since the non-verbal part of the message is more than fifty per cent, you need to be aware that gestures may be read differently depending on information in the knowledge filter of the recipient. Diane laughs when she recalls how she was cautioned in Australia not to use the thumbs-up gesture in her teaching: it has a very rude connotation!

Within our own culture, our socialization as males or females affects the information in our filters. Deborah Tannen offers a fascinating analysis of the difference between how men and women perceive the same behaviors from others in her book *You Just Don't Understand* (New York: Ballantine Books, 1990). For example if a woman says, "Do you want to go to the movies?" she intends to be initiating the issue for exploration. A male will hear such a comment as "Let's go to the movies," for he would not initiate such a conversation unless he had made a decision.

Women seek dialogue for rapport, Tannen says, whereas men use dialogue for position. When a colleague on staff mentions a new idea, a female is likely to recount a similar or matching example from her own experience. A male may well read this behavior as one-upsmanship on her part, even though this is not the intent. Different ways of filtering the same input!

Make yourself aware of such differences. Encourage staff to read books like *You Just Don't Understand* and initiate discussion among themselves. It is a fun way for staff to explore different perceptions. The more you can become aware of the ways in which you filter input, the more choices you have in how you can perceive a situation to keep your personal frustration low.

Learn to repeat what you hear in a form that inculcates the control theory concepts. Listen to what a person says, then paraphrase, "What I hear you saying is that what you are seeing right now is *(specific facts)* and how you are looking at it based on your experience is *(opinions/perception)*. When this happens you feel *(lack of caring, things are out of control, you don't have a choice)*.

Talk about the match or mismatch for the person between what is coming in and what is wanted. You might continue to paraphrase thus: "And what is happening now is not matching what you want to be happening in this situation. How would you like it to be? What outcome do you desire?"

Purposeful Behavior

Control theory teaches that "all behavior is purposeful." This means that no matter what a person does there is a reason for it. There are no useless behaviors. Every thought, action, feeling, and physiological change is generated for a purpose.

Reared in a stimulus-response society, you may believe that when another person disrupts your meeting your needs it is intentional and deliberate. You experience that person's behavior as causing you discomfort and you perceive your discomfort as an effect of that action on you. Control theory says that behaviors you perceive as disruptive to you are merely others' best attempts to meet their needs. To perceive another's actions as deliberately attempting to disrupt is not effective. It is better to perceive them as having a purpose for that person.

When children misbehave, educators may be able to forgive them the error of their ways because you grant to them the possibility that they have committed acts which are discomforting for you out of ignorance. With your colleagues, however, you may be less forgiving. You may tend to say, "He should have known better," or "She ought not to have done that." Control theory teaches that whatever behavior your colleagues are using is the best they can do at the time.

If they could have done better, they would have done better. Given their pictures of how the world should be run, they are at any given moment doing the best they can to get those pictures. Furthermore, the choice or behavior is avoiding a worse alternative. Can they learn a better way? Always. Will they? Not if you tell them to stop doing what, at this moment, is their best global choice. Not if you don't seek to understand and help them self-evaluate this choice before changing it. It is important, therefore, to understand that all behavior has purpose.

What is that purpose? The purpose in control theory terms is to close a frustration in the system. The frustration has arisen from an unmet need. There is a mismatch between what one wants to be happening and what one is perceiving coming from the world. The mind has created an intent. The control system is experimenting with ways to actualize that intent in the world. Every behavior is related to an attempt to get a specific picture.

You create what you want in your head, then you behave to create it in the world. What you create in your head, be it the perfect cake or the perfect school system, will pull from the world a match.

What Is Behavior?

What is behavior? Control theory says behavior has four components: action, thinking, feeling, and physiology. These components work together; there is always congruence to be found. For example, for every **action** there is a **thinking**, a rationale that sustains the action. When the action is in progress, there are **physiological** changes in the organism. The interplay between physiology and thinking brings a **feeling** readout which assists in evaluating the general state of the control system as it engages in the total behavior.

Behavior is not just action, but action is the component over which you have total control, if you are not paralyzed. You have moderate control over your thinking, although you can never have complete control or you could not reorganize and create. You have only indirect control over feelings and physiology.

As you alter your actions and thinking, your physiology will shift to match them. Your feelings can also be shifted, by changing the way in which you perceive a situation. We don't say, "You make yourself feel different," because such language would imply a direct causal relationship. Rather we understand that you do choose different thoughts, goals, and actions, and these choices give you a different feeling readout on the state of your system. An individual control system is designed to survive. It survives by creating behaviors to get the pictures it wants.

You Don't Do Something For Nothing

If this sounds a bit theoretical, let us look at some concrete examples. One of the ways to do this is to observe a strange behavior, then try to deduce its purpose. This is especially fun to do with perplexing behaviors which appear to have no purpose. For example, suppose at a party you see a person who appears to behave in a random, unorthodox fashion. You can't immediately understand why at one moment she is engaged in a conversation then abruptly makes an excuse to leave. She may be pouring a drink and leave the job half finished, or she may stop mid-sentence in a conversation. She appears disoriented to you, but she is not disoriented to herself.

However random it appears to you, her behavior is purposeful. She is either seeking or avoiding something. She is an input control system, and her maneuvering is intended to gain for her the perception that she wants. She is controlling not for her effort or movement or output but for the input she desires—the results she wants. You gain instant understanding when you discover that she is seeking a person or avoiding one. Or perhaps she is following an appetizer around the room, attempting to catch a chameleon, measuring the depletion of a bottle of alcohol, or trying to follow a conversation in the next room.

The moment you recognize the goal of a person's behavior, you gain a full understanding of that person's choice. All behavior is purposeful. You must only seek the purpose. Once you recognize your purpose, you can analyze your behavior, then you can self-evaluate.

It is important to understand that frequently you are unaware of your own intentions. You are driven by your internal pictures of how you want things to be. If these pictures are not at your conscious level, or if you deny they are within you, you may be confused about your own motivation. The question is the same whether you are observing another or observing your own behavior. What is the want? What is the intent? What input is your behavior getting you? Where do you shift courses? What is the purpose of this correction? What is the outcome? What expectation may be met by the behavior? It is great fun to use this process as a self-assessment tool.

Examples we have found in ourselves of purportedly useless behaviors are being late, forgetting things, and falling asleep at unexpected times. But there is a purpose for each of these behaviors. Being late and having others wait has been a test of our importance to the group. Forgetting has brought caring assistance from others. Falling asleep has been an interim solution to dealing with a conflict.

Are these behaviors useless? Not at all, even though they appear so at first glance. Each of these behaviors is our best attempt at the moment to avoid what our system perceives to be a worse situation. In the first case, it is going unnoticed without importance. In the second case, it is lack of being cared for. In the third case, it is possible estrangement from loved ones. **All behavior is purposeful.**

GETTING CLEAR

Getting clear is a central concept because control theory teaches that all of us are inherently self-evaluative systems. Self-evaluation means constantly comparing your pictures and perceptions to monitor the effectiveness of your behaviors.

When these actions are effective, your control system is in harmony, and the readout from that is a good feeling. When the readout from your system is a bad feeling, you have five choices.

First, you can change your actions to get harmony with the pictures you want. Second, you can change your intent by shifting pictures or creating new, attainable pictures. Third, you can exist in pain. Fourth, you can change your perception. Fifth, you can confuse yourself.

You can confuse yourself either about what you want, your true pictures, or about what you are doing, your actions. Such confusing is itself a purposeful cognitive behavior. It has the short-term payoff of pain reduction. By fogging either the want or the doing, you impair your system from giving you a clear readout. You have a diffuse feeling of discomfort but not the sharp feelings of fear, anger, or bitter disappointment. How can you be fearful if you confuse yourself about your actions and their import? How can you be angry if you keep your expectations low? How can you be disappointed if you deny your deepest wishes? Confusing can take such forms as over-rationalizing, denying, fabricating, or fooling oneself.

Although such confusion may be somewhat effective at times, an efficient control system depends on four processes. First, be very clear about what you really want.

Second, be scrupulously honest about what you are doing. Third, be intellectually cognizant of how you are choosing to perceive a situation. Understand the difference between the event and your perception of it. Fourth, let self-evaluation occur.

Monitor openness to receiving the feedback your system is giving at the physiological level. Sit with a moment of discomfort until you understand what your system is signaling you. Embrace generously the purposefulness of the behavior you have been choosing. Seek to understand the behavior: through this you can understand your need and how to meet it in a way that doesn't hurt others.

Self-evaluation is based upon knowing what you want and being honest with yourself about what you are doing. Being clear about your pictures and perceptions creates the conditions for self-evaluation.

SELF-EVALUATION

When you self-evaluate, you are always comparing the perception of yourself behaving in the world with your quality-world pictures of how you believe you should be behaving. The pictures you develop of yourself are based on the values you learn from others and then internalize.

It appears there also is an innate moral sense which humans have evolved over the years. We evolved this sense because it assisted us in surviving. Those who did not embody it have no descendants today.

> If Darwin and his followers are right, and I think they are, the moral sense must have had adaptive value; if it did

not, natural selection would have worked against people who had such useless traits as sympathy, self-control, or a desire for fairness and in favor of those with the opposite tendencies (such as a capacity for ruthless predation, or a preference for immediate gratifications, or a disinclination to share).

James Wilson, The Moral Sense, *p.23*

Learn to self-evaluate in this context of universal beliefs. Ask yourself, "How is what I'm doing aligned with what I know, want, need, and believe? Is what I'm doing getting me what I want? Am I being the person I want to be?" Then help your staff learn to do the same. Remember, you can teach self-evaluation best when you model it for others.

When you evaluate what you are doing, it is important to look at all four components of your behavior system. Look at your actions and your thinking or attitudes when you are doing these actions. Identify the feelings you have when you do these actions with these attitudes. Physical health also indicates whether what you are doing is really working. Are you fatigued all the time? Is there a high rate of sick leave? These factors can be used in the broad context to assess whether what you are doing is aligned with what you believe. When what you are doing is not a match with what you believe, you experience stress, or frustration.

Self-evaluation includes thinking about both what went well and what you would want to do differently next time. There are many topics you might consider when self-evaluating what went well. Ask yourself what you liked about what you did, said, thought, or felt. Evaluate whether what you did, said, or thought made a positive difference. Determine why it was important to you. Recognize the need—love, power, freedom, fun, or survival—that you satisfied. Consider how you helped other people meet their needs. Ask how it was a quality moment for you. Identify what values or beliefs were important. Think about what to do, say, think, or feel next time.

Summary

Control theory teaches that you are internally motivated by the pictures you have developed to meet your basic genetic needs for love, power, fun, freedom, and survival. Your feelings and physiology signal whether or not your actions and thinking are successful in getting the pictures you have chosen to meet your needs. When you have a mismatch between the pictures you want and what you perceive yourself getting in the world, you experience frustration. It is your internal motivation to reduce frustration that drives your behavioral system.

This behavior system is sometimes represented by a car analogy, with the wheels representing the components of total behavior—action, thinking, feeling, and physiology. Control theory teaches that your behavioral system is like a front-wheel-drive car in that you steer your front wheels, action and thinking, in order to control your back wheels, feeling and physiology. When you understand how you operate as a control system, you can choose which component of behavior to emphasize. No matter where you intervene, your whole behavioral system shifts.

Control Theory Practice

If you understand control theory, you will practice differently. As you begin to lead without coercion, roles and relationships change. Learn to rely upon influence rather than power, maximizing degrees of freedom for yourself and others. Intentionally reduce fear and coercion to increase need-satisfaction throughout your organization, to create conditions for the personal change you wish to encourage for getting started.

Use Influence, Not Power

The essence of leadership is influence rather than power.

> In evoking group performance over any considerable period of time, coercion is grossly inefficient....In contrast, if the leader can help people to see how both personal and group needs can be met by appropriate shared action, pressure is no longer necessary.
>
> *John W. Gardner,* On Leadership, *p. 184.*

Think about how you can lead by influence rather than by mandate. Understand the power of influencing others through modeling.

There are three kinds of personal power. The first is power over yourself, which can be gained by knowing your needs, understanding how you can choose to behave to meet them, and strengthening your physical body. The second is power over the inanimate world, which is the ability to impact on a thing using your mind and body. Any job where tools or computer technology are used falls into this category.

The third kind of power is influence over other people. Here you begin to build your emotional repertoire. Your emotions influence living beings. They don't influence tools, computers, equipment, or robots. They influence humans and to some degree other animals. You can also influence people with your ideas, by sharing information and resources which will help them, by acting in ways which you believe will help them, and by creating conditions within which they can help themselves.

MAXIMIZE DEGREES OF FREEDOM

Maximize degrees of freedom for yourself and others. Freedom is a basic human need. When people perceive they have no choice, they are frustrated. Offer your team a choice in the processes to be used. Show them freedom in how they might choose to perceive a situation, and grant the opportunity for expression of strong feelings. Help people understand that when there is no opportunity for freedom of action, there is still a choice of thinking and feeling to be created.

Increase freedom by acknowledging the value of diversity. This acknowledgment can include such areas as multicultural diversity, male/female perspectives, differences based on age, experience, and socioeconomic inequities. Recognize freedom of speech, freedom of religion, and freedom of political perspective. Although individual values cannot always be actualized in practice, it is crucial that you affirm the right to hold these diverse views. People have the right to think whatever they please, even though they may not have the right to act on what they think.

For example, a quality leader will not tell a group member it is wrong to espouse a belief in the inferiority of an ethnic group. A quality leader understands that this is the individual's point of view, but indicates that expressing this view is contrary to the social contact, and that there will be consequences for behaviors that violate others' freedom.

> By banding together and creating a shared reality, we reduce the size of the universe in which we live, narrowing the choices of goals and actions recognized as means toward goal achievement. The more of us there are, and the more closely-knit the society we perceive and accept, the fewer become the unused degrees of freedom and the higher becomes the likelihood of direct conflict.
>
> *William Powers,* Living Control Systems, *p. 227*

Create options to minimize this conflict for your teammates. Gain more personal freedom for yourself by understanding that everyone is already a self-evaluation system.

REDUCE FEAR AND COERCION

Dr. Glasser recommends that schools committed to quality begin by thinking of two or three ways to reduce fear and coercion. We agree, and we recognize that this mission involves a major shift from the traditional message most schools give students, "Do what we want, or we'll hurt you." Do you give this message to your students? Does your school give this message to your students? The following examples might sound woefully familiar.

Play respectfully on the playground, or stay inside for recess.

Remember your lunch ticket, or eat a cheese sandwich.

Walk in the halls, or go back and start again.

Do your homework, or go to detention.

Be on time for class, or your grade will go down.

Talk quietly in the lunchroom, or wait until it's quiet to go outside.

Staff also give this message to each other: "Do what the majority wants, or we'll punish you." How frequent is this message among the staff at your school? Here are a few examples we've heard.

Sign the contract to join the Quality School Consortium, or expect your next request to be denied.

Sign up for a district or school committee, or your co-workers will talk about how you are not a team player.

Come to the staff lounge in the morning for coffee and visiting, or some teachers will claim the school lacks staff unity.

Reducing fear and coercion is among the most difficult aspects of getting started, but it is indispensable. We suggest that you begin to create a less coercive environment by opening up the territory, asking "Does it really matter?" Other ways to reduce fear and coercion include management by "yes if," involvement, and role definition.

OPEN UP THE TERRITORY

Opening up the territory begins with inviting the dialogue of new ideas. No longer will certain questions be taboo because they recall previous administrative failures. You want to learn from your mistakes. To err is human; you need not expend valuable energy sweeping evidence under the carpet. No new idea is threatening because you know that you have the idea; it does not have you. You do not have to bow to current educational fashion if it does not suit you. You no longer engage in lavishly complimenting the emperor's robe while line staff whisper, "The emperor has no clothes." You need not be afraid to be found wanting. You have the creativity to design new robes, new suits—in fact, whole new ensembles for any occasion.

Where necessary, be willing to redesign yourself as well as your comfortable habits. Ask yourself the important question, "Does it really matter?" before you invest energy. Model maximizing degrees of freedom by controlling processes only as long as you need to control them, until the people you work with have developed themselves enough to take responsibility.

Yes, If...

Saying yes to every request would invite chaos, but saying yes as often as you possibly can will reduce fear and coercion. Often this means saying "yes, if..." or "yes, when...." The "if" is always if the needs of the organization can also be met or if your needs as leader are not jeopardized. Remember, people like to hear "yes, if..." a lot more than "no, because...."

"Yes, if..." offers the opportunity to problem-solve. "No, because..." discourages requests. You can always tell you are in a boss-management system when you hear staff say, "It's easier to ask forgiveness than it is to ask permission." This means that they have become discouraged trying to have input, so they have decided to do what they want and then feign confusion or apologize if confronted. "Yes, if..." management eliminates this behavior.

It is important to note that "yes, if..." is not effective when the task is too difficult. Staff can become skilled at solving complex problems, but to assign them at the outset can be discouraging. Give people solvable problems at the beginning and increase the challenge as the team gains confidence.

A problem can arise if you use "yes, if..." in an exploitative way, particularly when you know that an individual has a specific goal such as a promotion. You might be tempted to say something like, "Yes, we'll consider your application if you jump through these hoops." In this case you actually exploit the person by placing self-serving conditions in the way. This destroys trust. People begin to hide their aspirations so they won't be exploited. This is not "yes, if..." management.

To eliminate fear and coercion is the mission of quality leadership, but even reducing fear and coercion is an enormous task. Asking "Does it really matter?" and saying "Yes, if..." will contribute to this less coercive environment. So will attention to involvement and role definition.

Involvement

Another way to reduce fear and coercion is through involvement. There are two types of involvement: personal and role. Although leaders rely primarily on role involvement, personal involvement is essential. Personal involvement is finding common interests, finding out and caring about what is unique and special about each employee. To this end, the skilled leader draws on a wide variety of interests and a sense of humor.

Role involvement is always present in any relationship where there is a power differential. Role involvement is appropriate for outlining job expectations or in any discipline situation. If you can use role involvement to protect your personal involvement, you can discipline successfully without losing friendship or respect. Role involvement statements are:

My job is...

Your responsibility is...

The expectation is...

The rule is...

The policy is...

I'm in a position where I have to...

From my experience...

When you begin to feel yourself subtly threatening or persuading a team member, you are working too hard. You need to rely on policy. Use role definition and the "I need" statement to avoid being involved in a personal debate.

The "I need" statement is your clarification of what you want rather than what you don't want. The "don't want" can be too often perceived as criticism, whereas statements such as, "I need your reports in order to make budget projections," or "I need you to come to me if you want policy clarification," clearly focus the discussion at a professional level toward positive change. This is more productive than focusing on past mistakes which tend to leave the person with less sense of control and with a bad feeling. "I need" gives clear direction and an opportunity for successful collaboration.

Role Definition

Role definition is basically the job description. One of the tools which helps staff to feel secure in the change process is role definition. No one can be comfortable in an uncertain role. This is a special hazard in a changing organization, such as a quality school, where the role of the principal is dramatically changed or the role of the site team members needs to be created.

It is your job to be able to recognize when a person does not have a clear picture of what he or she is to do, and it is your responsibility to help develop and clarify the necessary vision. You may do this by several means:

1. Recognize that the problem is caused by the person not having a new picture of his or her role in the change process. This recognition will reframe a possible perceived conflict into a learning situation.

2. Ask questions to help people develop their own pictures.

3. Give information about the vision/goal/ purpose.

4. Connect people with others who can assist in clarifying management goals through their experience and perceptions.

In a quality organization, all staff work together to create an intrinsic mapping of each person's responsibilities. Such a prospect may seem frightening to anyone with a boss-management orientation who fears being blamed and punished, but that is not the intent of this process.

The intent of this process is for everyone to understand each other's job through clarification and negotiation among those who are affected. Skeptics might suspect people will try to diminish their duties, but this has not been our experience. We have found that people truly do want to do quality work. Only people who feel alienated by top-down managing will abuse the process. Most people are eager to figure out how to contribute.

In the Evergreen School District in Vancouver, Washington, the classified staff led the rest of the district in the process of role definition. They found the concept immediately useful, for it freed them from guesswork and streamlined communications between departments. Because the department heads so vigorously modeled the process by sitting down themselves with their staff and offering their jobs first to the process, others were quickly engaged, fear of the unknown diminished, and a cooperative spirit ensued. When school teams observed what office teams had achieved, they were encouraged to approach their principals to ask that the process be implemented for them. Jobs within the school that sorely needed definition were teacher assistants, resource teachers, and counselors—people who worked across several areas and sometimes had conflicting duties.

Clarify the system to reduce ambiguity. A gray area of authority is an accident waiting to happen. Since a control system is meant to be in control, people need role clarification to do quality work. Conduct dialogue with staff about "What is my job? What is not my job?" and "What is your job? What is not your job?" Figure 3 shows an example of role definition.

Role definition is a vital part of good leadership because it outlines powers and responsibilities for each person's position. There is no need to find fault or to defend. Excuses are irrelevant, for improvement is the goal. Role involvement is the key to both conflict resolution and effective discipline. It reduces coercion to permit collaboration.

Figure 3. **Role Definition**

Principal's Job Is...	**Teacher's Job Is...**
To create the conditions for change and renewal	To align what you do with what you know, want, and believe
To be a continuous learner	To be a continuous learner
To support as needed	To solve problems at the lowest level
To lead without fear and coercion	To take risks
To help gain access to best knowledge	To seek and use best knowledge
To self-evaluate	To self-evaluate
To do quality work	To do quality work

Principal's Job Is Not...	**Teacher's Job Is Not...**
To mandate change	To block change
To evaluate teacher	To evaluate principal
To do teacher's job	To do principal's job

School Example:

How to Reduce Fear and Coercion

Engage your team in dialogue about how to reduce fear and coercion in managing staff and students. Here is the result of such brainstorming in one district.

1. Talk continuously about the goals of the program and what you are trying to accomplish.

2. When people are successful, ask them to identify what worked for them in order to develop self-evaluation. Be sure to ask about both their actions and the thinking strategies they used to move themselves forward.

3. Build on the concept of each person as a teacher and a learner by asking people to share their learning experiences and knowledge with the group.

4. Welcome and solicit feedback. Lack of it is an indicator of fear. **Never** humiliate or belittle a person.

5. Talk about your thinking openly as a way to model how you are using control theory on yourself.

6. Welcome an opportunity to disclose a mistake in order to display (a) how you are generous to yourself and (b) how you think out a solution and restitution.

7. Model openness to feedback by accepting all suggestions without making excuses. State your picture if it is different, but try hard to come at it with interested curiosity rather than defensive righteousness.

8. Be certain that something positive happens as a result of feedback—either take an action or form a committee with a specific report date.

9. Don't be afraid to take a stand in the face of no feedback to your questions. State your position (need) and how you want to proceed in order to open up discussion or accomplish a short-term solution.

10. Whenever it is not possible for the group to reach consensus, the leader's job is to decide a course of action, giving your reason and setting a specific time the group will review it.

11. Where a yes is not possible, explain why the problem can't be solved as requested. Try to ascertain the need, so as to explore another way to satisfy it.

12. Open up the territory by asking, "Does it really matter?" and by saying, "Yes, if...."

MOVE FROM WANT TO NEED

A powerful control theory tool for replacing coercion with collaboration is the ability to move from the specific want to the general need. There are many possible pictures for meeting each need, but people get stuck on one specific solution which may be unattainable due to financial constraints or manpower limitations or timelines. They spin their wheels and argue and use killer phrases, which takes a lot of energy but doesn't solve the problem.

When you find people at odds with you or with one another about unattainable wants, you may become frustrated, discouraged, or defensive. You may be inclined to revert to the exercise of power to quell the controversy. This is normal, especially when you are getting started. But there is a better way. Moving from the want to the need increases freedom and involvement, while helping you maintain your balance and conserve your energy.

Remember that all behavior is purposeful, and prepare yourself for quality leadership by practicing the following questions. "Do I believe this person set out today to make my life miserable? Is this how I want to be feeling? Do I want to change how I'm feeling? Do I want to understand this person?"

If the answer is yes, then ask, "What do I think this person's want is? What is the need behind that want: love, power, freedom, fun, or survival?" Ask this question: "Should they not meet their needs?" The control theory answer will be that people do quality work when they meet their needs. They should meet their needs, but not this way.

It is important then to use your imagination: "If they gave up meeting their need in this way, what would that mean given the way they have things set up in their head? What would happen to those pictures?"

Ask yourself, "Do I want to lose this person's contribution to our process? Do I want this person to maximize professional freedom and become an effective problem-solver? Do I want to discourage or encourage? How can I keep my balance and help this person gain some control?" The answer is to move away from the unattainable want by seeking the need which must and almost always can be satisfied.

Dr. Glasser's concept of genetically encoded needs is a significant contribution underlying the practice of control theory because this is what allows discovery of broad common ground by moving from individual conflicting wants to universal needs. The questions to move from the want to the need are:

Why is it important to you?

How would it be better for you?

What would it mean if you got what you want?

What would you have that you don't have now?

These questions may generate different answers, but each answer will reflect one of the five needs: belonging, power, freedom, fun, or survival.

Learn to identify the needs of people by observing their behavior, by asking these questions and really listening to the answers. It is especially important, when they challenge you, to ascertain the intent of their questions, to avoid the trap of assuming what their needs are.

Teach this process, moving from want to need, to staff and help them do it, especially when they are spinning their wheels for unattainable wants. Suppose, for example, that a teacher asks you—the principal—for more computers. This is usually an unattainable want. Do you simply say so? Do you choose to become frustrated with the teacher who has put you on the spot, disheartened that you can't afford to grant the request? No, you seek the need behind the want. It may be different for different people, but there will be a common ground in some need area where you can find a way to satisfy the need when the want is unattainable.

Ask, "Why is it important to you to have more computers in the classrooms?" The response could be, "to be able to give more individual help to kids having trouble." You then might ask what it would mean to be able to do this.

Here is another example of a principal guiding staff from want to need. Teachers are worried about the behavior of children getting on and off buses. They want them to "shape up."

Why is it important to you?

We wouldn't be worried about the kids and wouldn't have to spend so much time supervising them.

How would that be better for you?

We could be preparing for class, doing what we were paid to do—quality teaching.

*What would it mean for you to have this prob-
lem solved to be able to do quality teaching?*

We'd be free from worry.

*So what we're looking at here is for you to have
freedom from supervising, so as to be in your
rooms preparing to do the quality teaching job
of which you know you are capable. How we've
solved it so far is by your being in the halls in
all breaks and after the end of the day, making
three or four corrections of behavior. Is it
working for us?*

"No," is the answer from some, but there are still
some who say yes, so the principal asks them to self-
evaluate again.

*If what you want is freedom from responsibil-
ity, to spend your time on quality work in your
classroom, are you getting it?*

No.

*But is it still important to have a safe environ-
ment?*

Yes.

The principal then frames a direction for the solution.

*Do we need to figure out a way for this to
happen without it being your sole responsibility?*

Yes, but it's not possible.

You will hear staff say, "We've never done it that
way. We haven't the time. We've tried that before. We're

not ready for it. Too hard to administer. Good ideas, but our school is different. All right in theory, but you can't put it into practice." You can become frustrated with your teammates, and vice-versa, until you learn the skill to move from the unattainable want to an attainable option which still meets the need. With the need identified, ask for self-evaluation.

> *But if you could have safety without having to leave your classrooms to assure it, is that what you want?*

Some say yes, some still demur. So the next question is, "If we do nothing, will the problem be solved?" They begin to make an assessment.

> *Can it get worse?*

Yes.

> *Is that what we want?*

No.

> *Do we want to change it?*

Yes.

Now there is the necessary commitment to plan a solution.

Always try to discover the disrupted need behind frustration. Usually you can help others figure out how to get what they need even though their specific want is not attainable.

For another example, a teacher may ask a principal to reduce class size. The principal can't at this time do what is asked. So the principal asks the teacher, "Why is this important to you?" or "What would it mean if you got what you want?"

The teacher answers, "Then I could give the children more individual time and get to know them." The principal reads the need as belonging and speaks to that need rather than to class size, saying, "I can help you figure out ways to get more contact with individual students, even though I can't reduce class size." Though you may think this approach won't work, it seldom fails to ease the situation. Everyone feels better when basic needs are addressed.

Now suppose that teacher had answered, "I feel I'm losing control with so many students to manage." In this case, the principal would answer, "It's important you feel in control of your class. How you would like to see this happen is by reducing class size. I'm not able to do that at this time, but I am willing to work with you and help you figure out what has to happen so you don't feel out of control in your class."

If you ask the fundamental questions, *Why is it important? What would it mean? How would it be better?* you will get to the need. Without this information, you may tend to inject your need into the scenario and work the plan in that direction. Half the time a plan doesn't work because it is directed to the wrong need. The plan itself may be fine, but a plan for more belonging will not help a teacher who is feeling out of control, any more than a plan for more control will help the teacher who is lacking belonging with students.

For example, someone may ask, "Why do we have to change this policy?" You might assume the person is desiring more power and that the question is a challenge. Only further questioning will confirm or refute this perception.

In order to check the assumption, you might ask, "What is your concern with this plan?" If the employee answers, "I don't know how I can get them to do what you are asking us to do," the need is probably power. "I think this change will destroy the spirit of collaboration among staff members," shows the need for belonging. "I don't feel we have any choice in the matter and I'm concerned that the decision limits our options," sounds like a need for freedom.

When you hear, "I don't feel the board cares about us," the issue is usually belonging. A comment such as, "We don't appreciate these changes being made without our input," indicates freedom. Comments which precede a power struggle may be, "I don't see how this will improve our output," or "Why do you ask me? I asked you."

Learn how you can modify your actions and perceptions to keep yourself in optimal balance. Recognize when you are running into a frustration and ask yourself the following questions:

1. What am I seeing or hearing right now that is not what I want? *(incoming perception)*

2. What do I want to be seeing or hearing at this moment? *(the input I seek—my picture)*

3. What is the need underlying that picture? *(love, power, freedom, fun, survival)*

4. How can I get what I need without aggravating others' frustration? *(a win/win solution)*

5. If I can't figure this out, am I willing to turn it over to the group for a creative solution? *(collaboration)*

6. If I'm not willing to turn this over for collaboration, what does my job require me to do at this juncture? *(role definition)*

Ask yourself:

1. What does this person need? What's behind this comment, question, behavior?

2. What are my expectations, policies, needs here?

3. What do I need to be saying or doing here to help meet this person's needs without violating my own needs?

4. Can we both get what we want?

HELP STAFF PLAN

There is a process for moving from the want to the need to build a plan for meeting the need. When there is a problem to be solved, know how to help your team (or yourself) make a plan. Ask questions that help people self-evaluate and then take action to get more of what they want. We have found that the Take Control Chart at Figure 4 is the most effective problem-solving tool to focus on the solution rather than the problem.

Teach it to staff and let them practice it in a thirty-minute session. Then everyone will have it in their repertoire to use for problem-solving. There are six parts and three levels to the chart. Parts one and two analyze the problem, parts three and four apply the control theory understanding, and parts five and six create the solution.

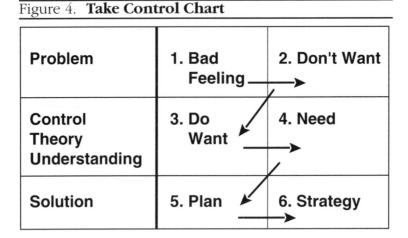

Figure 4. **Take Control Chart**

Problem	1. Bad Feeling	2. Don't Want
Control Theory Understanding	3. Do Want	4. Need
Solution	5. Plan	6. Strategy

1. Bad Feeling

Bad feelings are a signal that at the moment you are not getting the input from the world that you desire. These feelings indicate that you have a frustration or mismatch in your personal control system. This frustration is the impetus to change your behavior to get what you want or, in some cases, to decide to want something more attainable.

When you are getting what you want, you always have good feelings rather than bad. If you stay stuck at the bad-feeling level, you have little personal control. Usually you are hoping other people will sense the discomfort and come to your assistance. This may be effective for a short period, but in the long term people move away from you.

2. Don't Want

The moment you have a bad feeling, you can gain more control by identifying its source. The source is always a perception you do not want, something coming from the world that is not what you want to be seeing, hearing, smelling, tasting, or feeling. Identify exactly what it is that you dislike, and you have begun to gain the control necessary to solve the problem. For example, "I don't want her voice to be sounding that way on the phone. I don't like the spicy taste of this soup. I don't like the scratchiness of this sweater on my neck. I don't like the look he gave me." The moment you focus on what you don't want, you enter the thinking mode and the bad feelings reduce.

3. Do Want

Every don't want is the flip side of a do want that you have in your quality world picture album. Whenever you have a bad feeling, you can track it to some input coming from the world that is what you don't want. How do you know it is a don't want? Because you have previously formulated a picture of what you do want. This picture is coded onto your brain. You control for this picture and your system then alerts you when you have a deviation from it.

A key understanding in control theory is that your pictures are always positive for you. That is, every picture in your quality world meets at least one need for you. A picture which is negative for others may still be positive for you. An example might be eating cod tongues or chitlings or fish eyes or seal meat. These pictures may be positive for some people who welcome them. You may not have them in your quality world.

Your pictures are your pictures. If you want something, it must have a positive aspect for you. Every bad feeling indicates a "don't want" which originates in a "do want" picture. When you identify your do want picture, you move to level two on the Take Control Chart. You now have the control needed to solve the problem.

Level two is a thinking stage where you analyze what you need in order to take more effective control of your life. The moment you move from the don't want to the do want, you move from a reactive to a proactive position. Once you recognize the do want, you can self-evaluate. "Is it working for me to hold this want, this desire? Is it attainable? Can I achieve it without too much conflict with other wants I have? Does this want picture endanger others meeting their needs?"

At this point, if the do want is unattainable or antisocial, moving from the want to understanding the need that this want meets sets the stage for solution-finding. Remember, for every want there is at least one need.

4. Need

It is helpful to be able to identify the main need behind each want picture. This need can be cognitively identified. It can often be viscerally identified, that is, found by reading your body. Power feels like a push in the body. Often the hands are gesturing in a way to impact on the world. Examples include pointing, pounding, outlining, or rank-ordering in space. Freedom feels like the opposite. It feels like opening up the body. Gestures such as "off my back" or stretching longingly forward indicate freedom. Openness in the body is often indicated by palms up or open movement from one palm to the other. Belonging generally is felt in the heart area as a warm feeling. People may clasp their hands to their chest or almost hug themselves. Learning about the signals your body sends about your needs is helpful to self-managing.

The reason you want to know the need is that then you can substitute another want picture in the same need area to satisfy your system. Your system is amazingly flexible and easy to satisfy if you can meet your needs.

5. Plan

Once you understand what you need, you can plan to do one of the following.

1. Act upon the world to get what you want *(action)*.

2. Change your want picture to one which is within your grasp *(thinking)*.

3. Change your perception *(thinking)*.

4. Do nothing, which results in continued bad feelings.

Most people do not want to continue bad feelings. Therefore they ask for strategies to modify their actions or to change the way they are thinking about a situation.

To plan is to decide what you want to change. It can be specific, such as "I want some milk for my coffee," or it can be general such as "I need to have some more power in this situation."

6. Strategy

The strategy is not the "what" but the "how" to get what is wanted. At this stage, you can use others as resources to help you get what you need. The strategy answers when, where, who, which, how often, how much, how soon, etc. The strategy is confined to what you say you want to do. You may recognize this as the planning step of reality therapy. Eventually, staff will learn to do all the take control chart before they ask for help with a strategy.

School Example:

Diane Counsels Student Teachers

When Diane was supervising student teachers, at the beginning they would tend to stay stuck on the problem level, describing their bad feelings and talking about the don't want they were experiencing. She taught them to find their do wants from their don't wants. Then she taught them the five basic needs—belonging, power, freedom, fun, and survival—and they learned to identify which need was being disrupted.

By about the third counselling session, they would be able to approach her with the first five procedures completed. For example, a student teacher might say, "I felt angry *(1)* in the class today because I didn't want the teacher correcting me in front of the class *(2)*. What I did want was for her to talk to me in private *(3)*. I guess that's my personal power need *(4)*. I know what

I have to do, ask her for respect *(5)*. I don't know how to do it *(6)*. Can you help me?"

Teach staff—directly and through modeling—to move themselves along the Take Control Chart. Say to them, for example, "I was feeling frustrated *(1)* in the meeting yesterday because I didn't want it running so late *(2)*. What I want is for us to be finished in an hour and a half *(3)*. I guess it's my belonging need because I feel people disengaging after ninety minutes *(4)*. What I want is for us to be able to honor the time limits we set *(5)*. Can you help me figure this out? *(6)*"

In this manner a proactive leader can demonstrate how to conserve time on steps 1 to 5 and to focus on the solution instead of the problem. Once staff have an understanding of the Take Control Chart, they can use this problem-solving model as a strategy to help them align their classroom practices.

SUMMARY

Why is the control theory leader effective? How do you create the conditions for things to flow smoothly? What is the secret? The unseasoned leader can be trapped by the following:

1. Experiencing staff behavior as a personal assault.

2. Failing to interpret staff behavior in terms of their needs and objectives.

3. Perceiving a situation in win/lose terms: "One of us is going to lose this and it won't be me."

4   Escalating potential conflict by debating with staff or attempting to persuade them to give up their point of view.

5. Comparing staff unfavorably with others rather than referring to policy and expectations.

6. Acting without awareness of one's own needs and the expectations necessary to do the job.

You can avoid these traps when you know and practice control theory. With experience and maturity, you will accomplish the following:

1. Don't take negative behaviors personally.

2. Listen for the need expressed behind the behavior.

3. Help people to get what they need though it may not be what they originally stated they wanted.

4. Be aware of personal needs which must not be violated if you are to do a good job and feel content.

5. Be able to articulate the organization's needs as well as your perception of the staff's need in order to reframe a potential conflict into a problem-solving session.

6. Speak in terms of two different ways of looking at the same situation, not in terms of right or wrong.

7. Be able and willing to pass some of these skills along, mentoring those you supervise.

Learning control theory and becoming familiar with quality school ideas leads to personal change, and this change is reflected in management practices. As you strive to increase freedom, involvement, and clarity of expectations for yourself and staff, you create an environment which invites others to join in the change process. Specific strategies you can use for reducing fear and coercion and increasing commitment and creativity include "Does it really matter?", "Yes, if..." management, role definition, and involvement.

A great strength of control theory practice is reliance upon self- and group-evaluation to move from individual conflicting or unattainable wants to address general underlying needs which can be met. Control theory concepts applied in the Take Control planning process become part of the organization's problem-solving repertoire.

一視同仁

MOVING FORWARD

In this section we explore the process of visioning. In order to have a group vision, a fellowship needs to be created among group members. True fellowship, the prerequisite to group visioning, can only be attained when each member treats the others as equals within a structure that is not hierarchical. The proverb chosen for this part expresses the ideal conditions for systems change—everyone is valued as an individual and the environment is therefore safe for the expression of ideas.

MOVING FORWARD

Once you and some of your team understand the ideas of control theory and begin to apply them to your environment, you can move forward by engaging in the process of creating a shared vision. Although some schools and districts start with vision-setting before staff have internalized control theory, we find that schools with a stimulus-response perspective have difficulty with the processes of finding the common ground, reaching consensus, and moving from personal visions to a shared vision.

In those schools, when we talk about the importance of visioning, we hear, "We've already done that! Our district has printed our mission, outcomes, beliefs, values, and ethics." But when we try to explore this further, we find that staff cannot remember their vision statement. They thumb through their notes or send us to the office to find it written on the wall. It appears to us that they have not engaged in a meaningful process to decide, "What do we agree we want to become together?" If staff aren't able to articulate the expectations easily, the job is not complete.

The visioning question—"What do we agree we want to become together?"—propels the system change process.

In Getting Started, we focused on the personal change of perspective and practice that builds on information and paradigm shift and begins to open up the territory. With that process well begun, you are ready to use the reality therapy questions and group-process strategies to establish a social contract or vision for your organization.

It usually takes a school one to two years to get to this stage of the change process. Some may argue that creating a vision should be the first step, but we are suggesting that reducing fear and coercion comes first. Getting started rests on a very general vision of working towards quality through personal change, with the focus primarily on learning control theory. People need to try new things, to be flexible and not be afraid to make mistakes. They need freedom and involvement to develop trust. They need to be able to move together from the level of bad feeling to want to need to strategy. It is thus the personal and environmental change of control theory understanding that enables a system to move forward, to refine and develop a more comprehensive vision.

Moving forward in a Quality School means involving staff in creating their ideal world, creating a quality world picture or vision of their school, establishing a social contract of what kind of school they want to become together. Applying the principles of control theory and reality therapy, you can create conditions that foster genuine commitment and enrollment, so that the process of arriving at a vision will access the quality world. We believe the **process** of arriving at a vision is as important as the vision itself, and this process depends upon dialogue.

In many schools where there is difficulty moving forward, staff have read *The Quality School* and discussed it chapter by chapter and still have trouble. The problem is that individuals have different pictures of what the concepts in the book mean, and they may come out of such discussions polarized rather than united. An example of this is interpretation of the word non-coercion. Staff may polarize, with one faction thinking non-coercive means permissive, while another faction thinks it's merely a vehicle to abolish punishment.

The word punishment itself is subject to misperception. In the Quality School model, punishment is negative, discipline is positive. Punishment is when what happens to a child is unexpected, too severe, or accompanied by guilt or criticism. Some teachers say they disciplined a child when in fact they have punished. Others say they punished a child when indeed what they did was expected and fair, a consequence of the child's action.

The word persuade is another word which staffs debate. Some read the word as influence, others as a positive form of coercion. Another subject that a staff can debate forever is the concept of quality. Is quality dependent on external criteria derived by the group, or is quality an intrinsic feeling of great pleasure, or is it both?

Most school staffs have been trained to discuss rather than to participate in dialogue. They tend to debate rather than to understand each other's point of view, seek new information, and examine the implications of what they are learning.

Consider the principle of inclusion. Some people immediately read that as total homogeneity, and they resist this idea because it does not seem to them to honor individual needs. Others resist it because they think it means you never exclude students no matter how they behave. Because words are such an inadequate vehicle to convey pictures, their meanings must be explored in dialogue.

Invite your staff to engage in a vision-setting process that involves vigorous dialogue rather than mere discussion. What is the difference between discussion and dialogue? Discussion comes from the same root word as percussion, "quatio" in Latin, which means shake. "Dis" means asunder, so a discussion is a shaking apart in the conversation. Dialogue, on the other hand, means "speaking together."

The purpose of discussion is to have one's views accepted by the group. Even though people may take parts of other views to strengthen their own position, they still want their own views to prevail.

The purpose of dialogue, however, is to go beyond individual understandings and explore difficult issues from multiple perspectives. Through vigorous dialogue you merge your individual views into a richer pattern where the whole is greater than the parts.

When you understand control theory, you expect people to have different views. You value diversity. Rather than trying to persuade staff to accept your vision, engage staff in a process of vigorous dialogue using the reality therapy questions to find the common ground. We caution you that this process takes time, and we urge you to be patient with it.

In many schools we visit, both teachers and administrators rush the process. These are the schools where staff send us to the office to read their vision statement because they can't remember it. When these teachers tell us the process used to create their vision, these are some of the things we hear which indicate impatience.

- The outside consultant hired from business to help us with our strategic planning process facilitated our reaching consensus on our beliefs by yelling, "Decide, decide what you believe! Don't you know what you believe?"

- A small, elite group of people from the district were invited by the administration to go on a weekend retreat to create the district's vision statement, which was handed to us when they returned.

- After spending a half-day in dialogue about our beliefs, some of us expressed frustration, "We're wasting time! Let's get this over with!" The next time we met to continue the process, the planning team was worried about the brewing dissension. Rather than allowing another large block of time for dialogue, they started the faculty meeting one hour before the lunch break. We were told we had one hour to reach consensus on our beliefs, unless we wanted to have a shorter or later lunch.

If your school has a vision or mission statement, we invite you to self-evaluate whether your visioning process is complete. Do you know the vision statement? Do your colleagues? Are you excited about it? Are your colleagues? What process did your school or district use to arrive at your vision? Did you all hold on to your personal visions and add to them through a collaborative consensus-building process? Or did you have to compromise your personal visions? Are you revisiting your vision on a regular basis? Is it static or fluid?

The chapters in this section describe how to create the conditions for moving forward together on the journey to becoming a quality organization by creating visions and reaching consensus. Inclusion, involvement, freedom, trust, respect, autonomy—all these attributes of roles and relationships are essential for an effective visioning process. They all will be growing in an organization where control theory provided the platform for getting started. These strengths will be mobilized and enhanced for moving forward through structured processes for reaching consensus and creating visions.

REACHING CONSENSUS

Reaching consensus deserves its own chapter because it reflects a fundamental democratic belief that a solution devised by many has higher value than a solution proposed by an individual. Is this because many minds are better than one or is it because many minds involved in creating a solution are then involved in implementing it? Whatever the answer to this question, most people accept the premise that group wisdom is superior to individual wisdom.

Traditional training has accustomed us to think of group wisdom as majority rule. For becoming a quality organization, however, it is better to think in terms of decisions by consensus rather than by voting. To evolve as a consensus community is to believe in the value of each person's input to the group decision, even the input of the dissident.

One way to teach this is to invite dialogue about consensus using a T-Chart. Invite staff to brainstorm "What is Consensus?" and "What is Not Consensus?"

Figure 5. **What Is Consensus?**

Consensus Is	**Consensus Is Not**
All group members contribute.	A unanimous vote.
Everyone's opinion is heard and encouraged.	The result is everyone's first choice.
Differences are viewed as helpful.	Everyone agrees.
Everyone can paraphrase the issue.	Conflict or resistance will be overcome immediately.
Everyone has a chance to express feelings about the issue.	Only the most articulate members are heard.
Those who disagree indicate a willingness to experiment for a certain period of time.	Doubters stonewall or sabotage change.
All members share the final decision.	Majority rules, minority withdraws.

After such dialogue, Richfield High School staff summarized their thoughts about consensus this way:

CONSENSUS
Some things are given,
some things are negotiated, and
some things are agreed upon.

Becoming a consensus organization is one of the goals of a Quality District. As we strive to increase quality in the Richfield schools, we need a common understanding of what the term "consensus" means. Its dictionary definition refers to collective opinion or concord, general agreement or accord. This definition does not imply unanimity, a level of agreement which would be highly unlikely under most circumstances.

The conditions of most situations will dictate what determines general agreement. What will constitute consensus must be understood and agreed upon prior to addressing any issue. Determination of the fundamental values and beliefs of an organization may require significantly more than simple majority support. On the other hand, routine operational matters might be decided with a simple majority or even a plurality. It might not be necessary to require consensus for every decision, but the consensus-building process is essential to the development of ownership.

Consensus also implies that there will be reasoned dialogue concerning the issue at hand: differing points of view must be heard; the issue must be submitted to the screens of our beliefs, values, and best knowledge; participants should focus on what is substantial to the issue.

Consensus reflects what colleagues have agreed to create together. John Champlin emphasized that arrival at consensus then ethically compels each of us to act in a positive and supportive manner.

Consensus building is a critical component in aligning what we do with what we want, what we know, and what we believe.

REACHING CONSENSUS AT AN INFORMAL MEETING

There is a simple procedure you can follow to create conditions for reaching consensus. It incorporates control theory concepts, and it works to help staff move forward toward specific solutions as they develop consensus skills. Your job is to help the group set the stage, assign tasks, and give feedback.

Setting the Stage

Start the meeting with five minutes of positive discussion about what has been going well. Possible starters might include group reflection on the following subjects.

I am proud of...

I am looking forward to...

We've made progress in...

Assigning Tasks

Involve your group in taking responsibility for the meetings by asking for volunteers to facilitate movement toward consensus. Here are some examples of useful functions various members might perform.

1. Someone may volunteer to do the job of keeping the group on the solution. If people get emotional or get trapped into discussion about the past, this person asks:

    How would you like it to be?

    What can we do to help?

What do we think should be done?

What do we want to figure out before we leave?

What's our goal? What are we aiming for?

We have half an hour. How do we want to use that time?

2. Someone may volunteer to ask What style of interaction are we using now? (avoidance, accommodation, competition, compromise, collaboration—see "Getting Unstuck")

3. Someone may volunteer to look for coherence in the beliefs expressed, e.g., What do we all agree on? and also to look to put two wants together in one picture.

4. Someone may volunteer to encourage involvement of all the participants.

5. Someone may volunteer to work with the coordinator in forming the agenda, prioritizing it from group input, and keeping the group to the agreed-upon timeline.

6. Someone may volunteer to validate selectively the views expressed by others so they know they have been heard.

A group probably would not choose to monitor all these processes at one time, but it can be useful to focus on one or two at each meeting.

Giving Feedback

Adopt and adhere to solution-focused rules for giving feedback.

1. Look for areas of agreement.

2. Get the facts. Give input respectfully.

   The way I see it; the way it is for me...

   Your opinion; my opinion...

   I see it a little differently...

   My picture is; your picture is...

   Avoid *You're wrong, you don't know,* etc.

3. Listen to people who disagree until they've been heard. Don't argue with them. Try to understand their point of view.

When the discussion seems to focus on the problem use one of the following statements from *Restitution* to move toward a solution.

Is this getting us where we want to be?

What's our goal here?

Are we still on the problem?

Can we move to the solution?

What are we shooting for?

What can we do?

What's your plan?

What's your suggestion?

What do we want out of this?

Where do we want to be by four o'clock?

What do we need to have figured out by the end of this meeting?

Is this under our control?

Do we want to spend this much time on something we can't change?

What can we control here?

Can we think about this differently?

Is everyone participating?

What can we do to encourage participation?

How am I participating?

Am I talking too much?

Is saying nothing going to get me what I want?

Am I listening? Do I understand the person's need?

Am I being silent, then complaining about the outcome later?

Where are we on the levels? (Don't want, Do want, Plan?)

What's your picture?

Are we into personal issues here?

School Example:

Finding the Common Ground and Reaching Consensus

Judy's school discovered how important it can be to reach consensus, especially if there are strong feelings about an issue. Staff had strong feelings about signing up for school committees, and during the last few years it had been getting increasingly difficult to find volunteers to serve on these committees.

When Judy was a first-year principal, the secretary told her about the procedure for signing up for these school committees. On a teacher workday near the end of the year, the secretary asked, "When do you want to put out the sign-up sheet for next year's committees?" Judy knew there was something she didn't know by the way the secretary looked at her when she responded, "Oh, anytime, it's not a big deal!" Then Judy asked her the standard question she had learned to ask most often as a new principal, "What did you do before?"

The secretary explained that she used to announce over the P.A. system that she was putting the sign-up sheet in the lounge, then quickly return to the office before the stampede. Staff were eager to sign up for their first choice, and by the end of the day almost all the blanks were filled in by "happy volunteers."

She explained that things had changed, however, in recent years. She still put out the committee sign-up sheet on the teacher workday and made the announcement, but now at the end of the day only about half the blanks were filled by "complaining volunteers." People talked about how terrible it was that some people didn't volunteer. Some said people should "have to" volunteer. Last year some committees were dropped because nobody volunteered.

When they started planning for the following year, strong feelings surfaced when they got to the topic of school committees. They tried several group-process strategies for reaching consensus, but they always ended up talking about how people used to volunteer generously or how things were just not the same. When they shared their personal pictures about these committees, differences were viewed as hurtful instead of helpful. Diversity was resented rather than respected.

Judy has learned to use the power of self-evaluation to move things forward when they're not working. If she's facilitating a group and the group is stalled, she thinks about it as group-evaluation. She's careful not to judge or blame the group. First, she group-evaluates and asks, "What is the group doing?" and then she quickly self-evaluates and asks, "What can I do as a group facilitator to create the conditions for the group to reach consensus?" Then she self-evaluates in front of the faculty.

This is what her group-evaluation and self-evaluation sounded like with the faculty:

> I decided to spend some time thinking about how our last few faculty meetings have gone. It feels like we are "spinning on our back wheels." We've shared our pictures about some of these committees and we know we have some very different pictures.

"Could it be worse?" Yes, we could be silent like we used to be and then complain after the meeting. At least we know what people are thinking.

When I thought about the process we were using, I realized our discussions have focused on some of our most serious differences. Then I remembered hearing about how the Native Americans reached consensus. They began their council meetings by talking about all the things that they agreed on. They continued to focus only on items of agreement throughout their dialogue until eventually they had nothing to disagree about.

I am suggesting that we try that method of dialogue for our meeting today. Let's talk about the committees we think are important for next year.

They made significant progress at that meeting. People were pleased to reach consensus quickly on a couple of committees. When they sensed disagreement, they decided to postpone discussion of that committee and moved on to another area of agreement. At the next faculty meeting a teacher facilitated the dialogue with little conflict and completed the planning of committees for the following year.

REACHING CONSENSUS IN A MORE FORMAL SETTING

In other circumstances, you may also want to help a board or other more formal group learn to reach consensus more fluently. It is desirable that all members present a united front on issues they decide and no members indicate that they voted against it in order to get off the hook on a controversial issue. A decision made by fifty-one percent of a board lacks the support necessary to be taken into the community.

Vince Deveney, Superintendent of Truckee School District, claims that decisions can be made by consensus if you provide board members with pros and cons of an issue in advance of the meeting and if you sustain dialogue at the meeting to include all perspectives. To help your board understand this, and to give them an opportunity to learn to do more talking and listening, we suggest you offer a workshop on the functioning of the board. In this way, the new board members can understand their role in the meetings, and each year the board will get stronger as it reviews its improvements over the previous year.

See if your board can agree on some of the same task assignments and feedback rules you use in your more informal meetings with staff. Propose they try a systematic process such as the one outlined here.

1. The leader will prepare an agenda in advance of the meeting and circulate it to the members, attempting to identify each issue for information, discussion, or decision, according to the guidelines established by the group, perhaps in their annual workshop.

2. The chairperson will go around the table and invite each person to speak on issues that need a decision. There will be an attempt to reach consensus. The guidelines for consensus will be followed. It is important in the process of consensus that the majority work very hard to understand the position of the minority members on an issue.

3. The majority will not attempt to argue the dissenting members out of their concerns, but rather will listen to understand what their reservations are about the decision to be made, until dissenters feel they have been understood. Often the dissenters will concede to the early majority, even though they remain unconvinced. By following procedures for consensus, it also may occur that the entire majority will be converted by a single dissenter who is carefully heard and fully understood.

4. Members will attempt to speak out on issues and will give their opinions when the chairperson goes around the table.

5. Members will show respect for each other's opinions. They will use the process that was agreed on for feedback.

6. Take a straw vote from time to time to clarify who dissents. Only if absolutely necessary will the issue go to a majority vote.

DESIGN BACK

In formal or informal settings, designing back can help a group reach consensus by focusing on where they want to end up. Get agreement from the group on the end point sought by seeking the common ground. Some questions to ask are: *What do we all agree on? Do we all agree that what we're doing now is not getting us what we want? Do we all agree that a change is necessary? Do we all agree that we want things to be better for kids? Do we agree we can't do it without working together?* By starting with areas of agreement, you can help the group become aware of the beliefs they hold together.

Control theory teaches that you control for input, not output. If you seek input that will affirm your common purpose, begin a meeting by focusing on the input you want to create. This input will then be the outcome of the meeting.

Design back. Talk about where you want to be at the end of the meeting. What will characterize the solution you desire to create? What would be the best possible outcome for all parties? Be specific, ask: *What do we want to be better when we leave this room in two hours? What do we want to be thinking about our group process? How do we want to be feeling as we walk to our vehicles? What do we want to be saying to each other as we drive away about how we have treated each other in this meeting? What kind of participant do you want to be? How do you want people to view you at the end of this process? Do you want to be a facilitator or a blocker? If you choose to be a facilitator, what will you need to be thinking, saying, and doing in this meeting?*

You may want to spend five to ten minutes letting people speak to each other in small groups about the outcome they seek and the person they want to be in the process. This is particularly important if the issue to be discussed is a controversial one.

Another technique for designing back is to ask the group to visualize the worst possible outcome. This is a good technique to use if the group is slow to get moving. The reason this question is easier for them to answer is explained in control theory. Always your brain gives strong negative signals when what you are getting is not what you want. People always know what they don't want. From there they can move to what they do want. If you have taught them the Take Control Chart, they have learned to do this for themselves.

Focus intentionally on the positive outcome you want. If you focus on the negative outcome you fear, you tend to create that situation as input from the world. For example a coach who says to a basketball player, "Whatever you do, don't be distracted by the noise of the crowd," is creating the condition for what he does not want to see. The subconscious brain does not read the negative. It reads only "noise of the crowd." Therefore it is important if you use the question, *What don't we want to happen?*, that you close the process by refocusing on what the group does want to happen. Once you know what you want and who each of you wants to be in the process, you can create the input you want and your desired outcome.

CORE BELIEFS: FINDING COMMON GROUND

Consensus skills are developed through the structured problem-solving processes we have described. As they grow stronger, these skills are vital to identifying the common ground of core beliefs at higher levels of perception. Every organization needs to establish its purpose and its goal. From this evolves its mission statement, the vision we address in the next chapter. Here we define a procedure for identifying the core beliefs which generate purpose. Remember throughout this process to follow the consensus procedures you have practiced in problem-solving: set the stage, assign tasks, give feedback with care.

In order to move toward identifying the higher purpose, begin to ask questions at a low concrete level of perception: *What do we want to be seeing and hearing in our program? In a good workplace what would be happening?* These questions will pull out the very specific pictures that people are filtering for when they go into the workplace each day.

Collectively make a list of what the team wants to be perceiving. The collective list will be more extensive than any individual list, and from this list you can identify elements which the group holds in common. This very specific common list will form the foundation for higher level, more philosophical, shared goals. It is easiest however, to go first for agreement on concrete perceptions, because pictures are likely to be similar at this level.

After eliciting the more concrete perceptions, the second step of the process is to ask for the meaning of each perception. Ask the group, *If this which you want to see/ hear happens, what will that mean to you?* The answer to this question can generally be categorized into one of the need areas of belonging, power, fun, freedom, or survival.

For example if a person says, "I like to see management having coffee with staff," the answer to the question "What would that mean?" might be: "It shows they care," which denotes belonging; or "It shows they respect us," which could be tied to power. "I wouldn't feel segregated from the big brass in the basement, I'd feel mobile," might suggest the need for freedom.

The same concrete picture may meet different needs for different people, and that is all right. The main thing is to be sure that no picture selected by the group is in violation of any one individual's needs.

The next step is to use a class-meeting format to ask the questions from Figure 6, Deriving Core Beliefs. These questions address the issue, *If you were seeing what you want to be seeing in this organization, what would that say about us?*

When this dialogue is complete, you should have quite an extensive list of beliefs. The final step is to reduce this list to common denominators reflecting higher values. Ask:

If you had to choose five or six crucial beliefs upon which to build this organization, which of the above would you not want to leave out?

Which one is absolutely essential to what we believe about how we want to be?

Can any other of our stated beliefs be subsumed under this one?

What is the next belief you would hold on to?

Is it different from the first one? Does it subsume any others?

What is the third different belief that is not covered by the other two?

Continue this process until the group has derived the minimal numbers of beliefs possible to describe their values. These few statements become the core beliefs of the organization.

Figure 6. **Deriving Core Beliefs**

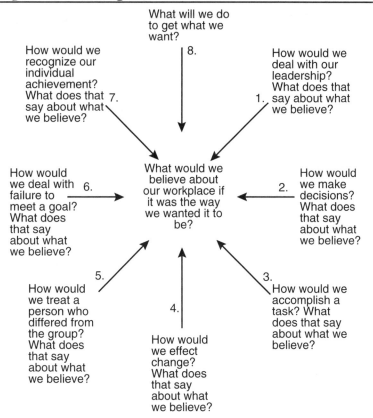

Chelsom Consultants, Ltd.

Seeking in this way to discover common ground, staff not only reach consensus but improve their skill for doing so. With consensus about core beliefs and increased trust in the process and in each other, the group is ready to move the organization forward toward more effective problem-solving, non-coercive planning, and inclusive decision-making.

School Example:

Moving Forward through Crisis

Here are two examples of schools where consensus skills are well developed and used to keep moving forward when crisis might otherwise threaten. You will note how the process is facilitated by movement between higher and lower levels of perception.

One district was in turmoil after a racist comment by a well-regarded teacher. This district used the crisis to work with community members to develop multicultural dialogues. They viewed the incident as an opportunity to educate a student body which was not very ethnically diverse. They vowed to seek more staff from minority groups. The questions which assisted them to move through this crisis were questions at the systems level of universal beliefs. "What do we believe about equality? What kinds of persons do we want to be in handling this crisis?" They also sought consensus at the principles level: "How can we find a solution which does not divide our community? What does this say about our exit outcomes?" At the program level, they asked, "What strategy will we use? How would a Quality School resolve this?"

Another district faced a crisis which originated when very inappropriate posters were published by a group of athletes challenging another group to competition. As a consequence, the principal cancelled the school event. Since the protocol was quite clear, the incident could have ended there, with consensus about the resolution. Instead, using this as a starting point, parents, board, teachers, and students elevated their dialogue to examine their values about discipline in the district. They moved toward consensus at higher levels of perception with questions like these. "What does this tell us about the culture in our school? What do our students believe about respecting themselves and others? How has our competitive spirit gotten so out of hand? How does the school's discipline help students examine their beliefs? How can we view this experience as an opportunity to grow rather than as a discouragement? How can we adults model our beliefs by seeking our common ground without castigating each other?"

SUMMARY

The quality organization moves forward by consensus, with limitless patience for the dialogue which creates it. It is essential to work from a level of perception where consensus can begin. If there is no agreement at the principles level, move the questioning to the systems level of universal beliefs or to the program level of how to proceed rather than what you believe.

Sometimes people may agree how they want to act even when they can't agree on the principles that such actions would serve. Sometimes people can agree on what they believe more readily than how to implement it. In either case, the desired consensus arises from existing common ground as a result of patient dialogue. Using consensus processes for problem-solving will keep an organization moving forward toward its quality vision.

CREATING VISIONS

Creating visions is the goal of moving forward, releasing the energy locked into our dreams of how things might be.

> First of all, a vision is greater than ourselves. Vision is always about greatness. A vision expresses our values and what we hope to contribute. Vision is about creating an organization that expresses our deepest values about work, family, achievement, or community. Vision transforms momentary strategies into a way of life. Vision engenders change. Vision is creating an ideal, preferred future with a grand purpose of greatness.
>
> *James Mapes, "Foresight First", Sky, p.96*

Vision is about others, idealistic, from the heart, authentic, and extraordinary. Most of us are reluctant to share our dreams because they seem so unattainable and we are afraid people will laugh. But your vision should be unattainable, it should be a shining beacon which pulls you forward with its fire.

We emphasize the importance of shared visions emerging from personal visions. We know that this process takes time, but it is **sustained** involvement which fosters enthusiasm and commitment. Visions that are truly shared take time to emerge, because they grow as a by-product of interactions of individual visions.

Experience suggests that genuinely shared visions require ongoing conversation where individuals not only feel free to express their dreams, but also know how to listen to each other's dreams. Out of this listening, new insights into what is possible gradually emerge. Listening is often more difficult than talking. It requires extraordinary openness and willingness to entertain a diversity of ideas.

This does not imply that personal visions are sacrificed "for the larger cause." Rather, it means that multiple visions coexist until a course of action emerges to transcend and unify individual visions.

Dr. John Champlin, former Superintendent of Johnson City Schools in Johnson City, NY, outlines several important aspects of a clear and compelling vision statement:

> The vision statement to be effective requires opportunities for influence and collaboration on the way to consensus.
>
> The vision statement is constantly open to influence and review as better knowledge makes new opportunities possible.
>
> The vision statement is a working guide for all decisions.
>
> The vision is seen as part of becoming, an aspiration and a challenge and never a prescription.
>
> The leader has assured that everyone is a player and contributor. Feedback prevents anyone from becoming a spectator.

The vision statement arises from and also fosters involvement. In any organization it is important that the people who work together have a strong sense of their common purpose. The common purpose is expressed in a shared vision statement. The shared vision is the picture of what the group wants to become together.

The vision statement should develop with all staff collaborating. The more inclusive the vision-setting process, the more ownership the staff has. Only when you truly have the courage to share your hopes and dreams with each other will you build together the energy to create jointly your shared idealistic vision. In this chapter we offer you some structure and examples, this time for applying control theory to creating visions.

USING REALITY THERAPY QUESTIONS

Control theory is a broader concept than reality therapy. It explains why reality therapy works and also why other therapies can be effective. Reality therapy intervenes at the thinking-doing level, while other therapies intervene at the emotional level (e.g., aggression therapy) or the physiological level (e.g., drug therapy).

As you experience the process of organizational change and move forward toward a shared vision, it is important to stay at the thinking-doing level so you can share and absorb information. When you attempt to control one another emotionally, you move apart, seeking freedom. This is not conducive to group endeavor; it disrupts the involvement which produces shared visions.

By keeping yourself at the thinking-doing level, you can learn to choose behaviors that get you what you want as a group. You keep yourselves in balance and you feel good. This permits the continued involvement and energy needed to create a shared vision. This is not to advocate any intention to offer therapy as part of organizational change. It is rather to adapt a powerful, systematic, thinking-doing process to the frame of reference for quality leadership.

Reality therapy uses four simple questions that lead to change.

1. *What do you want?*

2. *What are you doing?*

3. *Is it working?*

4. *What is your plan to get more of what you want?*

The intent of these questions is to reach an evaluation: *Does your present behavior have a reasonable chance of getting you what you want now and will it take you in the direction you want to go?* Just as these questions lead to change in individual clients, these questions also can lead to significant change in a district, a school, a faculty, a principal, or a teacher. Discover the power of these questions, become confident in using them continually to invite individuals to self-evaluate and teams to group-evaluate, using these questions to create their vision for change.

In 1986 Diane worked with the Johnson City leaders teaching them control theory and reality therapy. As they worked with the questions of reality therapy—*What do you want? What are you doing? Is it working?*— it became evident that there were several levels to each of these questions. They discovered that wants are tied to needs and needs are tied to beliefs.

What you want/need/believe is derived from what you know, your experience. What you experience is a result of your new learning and your testing of new learning through practice. Together your new learning and your experience with it becomes your best knowledge. Pooling individual best knowledge yields group best knowledge upon which to make decisions. The group best knowledge then can be used to evaluate what you are doing to see if it is working for you.

In Johnson City, we talked about the beliefs being high up in the perception system. For example, a common belief that we discussed was the belief so basic to control theory, "You can't control other people." This belief is related to people's need for freedom to become, and to our want for them to be self-disciplined, to meet our need for freedom from responsibility for their actions.

To depict the connections among wants, beliefs, experience, and behavior, Al Mamary and colleagues in Johnson City devised the Success Connection, which is a keystone of the Outcomes-Driven Development Model. The reality therapy questions are the core of the Success Connection. Significant change can happen when these questions or the Success Connection are used to create a vision.

USING THE SUCCESS CONNECTION

A simple definition of the Success Connection is aligning what you do with what you know and want and believe. This process involves all staff reaching consensus on six loose/tight connectors—purpose, beliefs, outcomes, values, ethics, and knowledge.

These six connectors create the ideal world, and they serve as a screen used to align what a district does—a screen to align school and classroom practices. The loose/tight connectors serve as points of consensus. Each of the connectors prescribes conditions for appropriate behaviors and aligned decision making.

Start with the question "What do you want?" The want is usually stated in concrete terms. For example, "We want students to have eighty percent mastery of content," or "We want fewer than five students sent to the office in a day for behavior disruption."

It is important to be specific to know where you want to end up. Don't try to move on a don't want because it will have no energy. For example, planning "so students don't pass knowing only fifty percent of the material" is discouraging. Whenever you consider changing what you want, ask the questions, "Why do we want to change this? What belief is behind our desire? What exit outcome are we striving for?" At this stage you move from the concrete to the abstract.

You move to this level in order to establish agreement, as you did in reaching consensus about core beliefs. When you discuss the beliefs, you are aiming for the highest level of perception, the system of values. This level holds what you believe about the world and how people treat each other. The universal values are at this level.

Some of the beliefs you will find are beliefs about fairness and quality work. The belief that you can't control another, that you can only control yourself, is at this level. The belief that humans are intrinsically motivated to learn is at this level.

Every want can be tracked back to either a need or a belief. A belief is higher than a need. Once the belief is established, invite staff to talk about the needs that would be met if they got what they wanted and valued. If fewer students were coming to the office for discipline, for example, it would mean that they were more self-disciplined. If this were so, teachers would have more control. Students would be meeting their personal self-esteem goals, and adults would have more freedom.

It is important that you assist the group in moving through different levels of discussion. It can be very frustrating if various members of the group are operating at different levels of perception. You can end up having parallel conversations and no common ground. With questions, you can help the group move from the concrete want to explore the abstract beliefs.

The process for using the Success Connection questions can be summarized in the following way. Ask people what they want *(what you want)*. Look for overlapping pictures in their quality worlds. Ask them why they want what they want, to establish the beliefs *(what you believe)*. Then relate the beliefs back to basic needs. When this is finished, it will be quite clear to the group the direction in which they believe it is right to move.

Figure 7. **Success Connection**

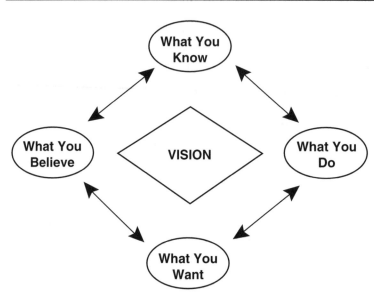

Al Mamary, Johnson City Schools, 1986

Then ask people what they know *(what you know)*. Explore the resources in your group. What experiences have people had with this concept? What have people read or heard from others? Collect all the experience in the group in an open-minded fashion.

Establish what you collectively know, your best knowledge. When you are at this level, you are dealing once again with facts which can be verified.

The final step is to develop a specific action and thinking plan to solve the problem *(what you do)*. Decide what you will do, how you will do it, and how you will be thinking about it as you take on the challenge.

Johnson City leaders were exceptional in their ability to take the control theory knowledge and the reality therapy questions and check them against their beliefs. They gave Diane an exhilarating experience of vigorous dialogue to self-evaluate and to group-evaluate.

Richfield Public School District also used the Success Connection to develop a vision. The process for reaching consensus was time-consuming, but they realized the **process** was as important as the **product**. The process involved dialogue between teachers, administrators, and parents. It extended over twelve months and included nine drafts. The result constitutes Appendix A.

CREATING A SCHOOL VISION

Even if a district has established a vision, it is important for a school to develop its own vision. Faculty use the district's loose/tight connectors (purpose, beliefs, outcomes, values, ethics, knowledge) as a screen to align their school's vision.

Begin by developing a personal vision and inviting everyone else to do likewise. When you candidly present your personal vision to the group, your message is, "I want to share my vision because I want you to influence it, own it, be excited about it." The vision is a picture which others are invited to contribute to and influence.

The outline of this first vision shared is clear, but everyone can influence it. Invite others to share, to contribute to building something everyone can rally around. People will listen, then question, and partake of each other's excitement. Ask, "Is the vision attractive to you so that together we can make it happen? We can become what we want to be together."

Figure 8. **Judy's Vision Web**

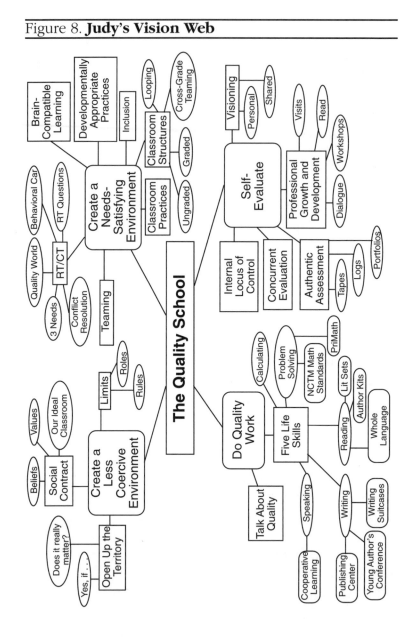

School Example:

Judy's School Visioning Process

Judy tells how her school created their vision. Staff were invited to reflect on their personal visions in preparation for a teacher planning day. Judy prepared her vision using the concept webbing shown in the diagram at Figure 8.

The four main parts reflected Dr. Glasser's ideas about a quality school: (1) reduce fear and coercion, (2) focus on quality work, (3) provide for self-evaluation in a (4) needs-satisfying environment.

Her vision of creating a needs-satisfying environment included practicing and teaching the concepts of control theory and reality therapy along with some education-specific ideas about students' needs. Her vision of quality work included ways of teaching the five life skills that Dr. Glasser outlined in *The Quality School Teacher* (New York: Harper Collins, 1993). Her vision of self-evaluation included ways to help staff and students self-evaluate.

At the beginning of the meeting Judy explained her personal vision to the faculty. Then teachers shared their personal visions in small groups of three or four people. They talked about how their visions were similar to and different from her vision and each other's. Then two small groups combined to form a larger group of six to eight. After further dialogue about their personal visions, the entire faculty outlined the important components of their shared vision.

School Example:

A Simple Beginning

Judy's was a complex process, but visioning also can begin very simply. Tom Johnson, the principal at Placer High School in Auburn, California, started his school's visioning process by making this very simple, but very provocative speech.

Change? You bet. Heraclitus said "the only constant is change." He was given to understatement. Should you be worried? Should you be desperate? I hope not, and I hope so. A little change goes a long way to renewing people, to motivating people. The key is a little change, as long as it doesn't affect me, right?

One of the first changes you will notice is that I will encourage people to share leadership responsibilities in critical positions on staff. I like to see "co-ing" as much as possible: co-chairpersons, co-athletic directors, co-activity directors, co-coaches, team teachers. When people share authority, they become more aware of the problems and responsibilities of decision-making, and they also burn out at a far slower rate, or get "comfortable" at a lot slower rate.

I'd also like to see us behave like a flight of honkers. In the honker model, that goose winging it at the point doesn't stay there for ever and ever, but falls back and lets another share the lead position. All in the flight share in its direction. For many teachers, opportunities to lead never surface in a lifetime. They should.

I will also encourage departments to look at themselves in relationship to leadership: are there sacred cows?

Sugar daddies? Mandarins? Elitists? Are there unwritten "hands-off" norms? Are there opportunities for all department members to access the courses that are viewed as requiring leadership? People don't get stretched and grow when they are stunted with one preparation for twenty years. As Roland Barth says, "The only difference between a rut and a grave is the depth of the hole." Yes, those should be interesting meetings.

VISION OF A QUALITY SCHOOL

One thing we have learned in helping schools create visions is to keep them simple. As trainers going into a variety of districts, we have encountered a plethora of exit outcomes that seem to overlap in meaning and melt into each other. Sometimes schools are assigned exit outcomes which they did not participate in deriving. Often when we ask people, "What are your exit outcomes?" they say they're on the wall or they flip through pages to find them. Here are some of the expectations we commonly find in districts moving toward quality.

Acquire knowledge	Positive Concern for Others
Respect	Quality Work
Self-Esteem	Caring
Lifelong Learning	Self-Directed
Maximized Learner	Responsible
Participating Citizens in a Democracy	

 Each is good. Each is important. But they tend to overwhelm or confuse or bore people because they are so abstract. One of the ways to simplify the definition of targets or goals we strive for is to ask parents what they want for their children. Diane has done this with over fifty groups and heard very consistent answers.

Figure 9. **Parents' Wishes**	
I want my child to...	
...be safe	...learn
...be happy	...think critically
...like school	...be responsible
...read	...cooperate with others
...have friends	...have the latest technology

As these answers come from parents, she lists them in three corners which can be joined to form a triangle (see Figure 10). The three corners represent the three most important tasks of education: (1) Achievement, (2) Self-Esteem, and (3) Responsibility.

Inside this triangle of parents' wishes is a smaller triangle which represents the basic psychological needs we are trying to help children meet. In the middle is an even smaller triangle which represents survival needs. These matter to us because it is hard to teach a child who is hungry, tired, or sick. When we are meeting these basic needs we have enormous pleasure. There is fun in quality learning. There is fun in quality friendships. There is a fun component to feeling free. So we join the corners by a ring representing the fourth psychological need of fun.

Figure 10. **Tasks of Education**

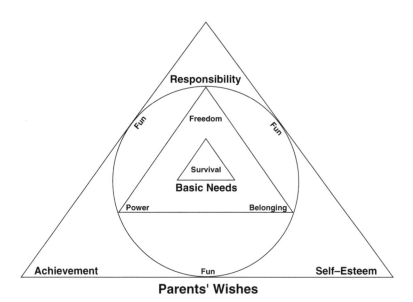

Parents' Wishes

When learning partners look at the three corners of this school triangle it demystifies the exit outcome process for them. They realize there are three main targets to keep in sight.

Side one—Academic Corner: quality learning encompasses instruction, curriculum, and assessment. Side two—Social Corner: cooperation results in respect for self, others, and our environment. Side three—Citizenship Corner: democracy depends upon how decisions are made and how the power of the individual is balanced with the desire to belong to a group.

Figure 11. **Quality School Vision**

Teachers and community people will recognize that schools have tended to cycle through these corners in about five-year terms. Examples are the Back to the Basics movement, which focused on the academic corner; the Confluent Education movement, which focused on the social corner; and the Assertive Discipline movement, which focused on the self-discipline corner, asking how to influence children to behave the way adults want them to. Each of these movements has a limited life cycle.

We believe the Quality School focuses on all three corners. We want to see all these three balls in the air at once. Try to address all the corners simultaneously. Not everybody can do every corner, but someone in each school needs to be working on each corner.

Seeing that what parents want for their children corresponds with what educators want for schools is a big relief. It means that educators are aligned with parents, whom W. E. Deming calls the external customer.

In this model the outer triangle also reflects what society wants from schools. These terms are high-minded and philosophical. They express the hopes and dreams of the nation for the kind of citizens they hope schools will help children become. Society wants citizens who can make capable contributions, who can work as a team, and who can make democratic decisions.

In fact Carl Glickman, in *Renewing America's Schools* (San Francisco: Jossey-Bass Publishers, 1993) states that the development of informed citizens of a democracy should be our main agenda. It does make sense that they become informed by being educated and learning to respect themselves and others in interacting with many kinds of people in the school and learn to make democratic decisions by balancing the freedom of the individual to achieve with the greater good of the group.

Each of the corners of the Quality School triangle corresponds to one of the principles which Dr. Glasser sets out for the Quality School. Corner one, the academic corner, is also the corner for quality work. Quality work comes from the worker being actively engaged in doing the best possible job. Corner two, the social corner, is also the corner for self-evaluation. In order to self-evaluate, people need to respect themselves and to be in touch with who they want to be. Corner three, the self-discipline corner, is the corner where people decide how they are going to work with others and what limitations they will accept from the group to be part of the group.

When you get quality work, self-evaluation, and self-discipline in the least coercive environment, you will have a quality organization, where each person can have power, belonging, freedom, and fun. When a school asks about becoming a Quality School, we talk about *what* to do (seek quality work), *who* will do it (students and teachers who have high self-esteem and can self-evaluate), and *how* it will be done (through a true democratic process).

Dr. John Champlin also suggests a congruent vision. His vision of a Quality School includes three components: children learn how to learn successfully; children keep their positive self-esteem intact; and children have choices and options for being successful in the learning process. His three ideas correspond to the three sides of our triangle:

Achievement	Children learn to learn successfully
Self-Esteem	Children keep their positive self-esteem intact
Decision-Making	Children have choices to be successful

In developing a Quality School vision, we suggest a close alliance with the people who receive your services—the parents. If you ask parents what they want, they will tell you they want useful learning, children to feel good about themselves, and children who behave. They will always give you some form of these three goals because parents are human, and all humans are motivated to meet their needs to survive, to be successful, to be loving, and to be free.

Society's goals, reflected in the decisions of the legislature, are to help people survive, be successful, be caring, and be free. Teachers want to be successful and caring and free. Students want to be successful and caring and free. Society knows that people who can balance survival with success and caring and freedom are not people who hurt each other. We all have the same agenda.

SUMMARY

As your organization moves forward in the change process, the fundamental principle of self-evaluation increases in scope. During the vision-setting stage, the group is developing its want pictures, against which will be evaluated all subsequent plans and perceptions as the organization seeks alignment of practices with beliefs and values. Whether following a Reality Therapy model, Success Connection model, or some other, the visioning process depends upon dialogue.

The process for change to become a quality school can be confusing. One doesn't know which program to use. Quality School? ODDM? TQM? Responsibility Training? It is especially difficult because program names are in flux. The good news is that they have more in common than they have different. All are intended to improve communication between the givers and the receivers of service.

All emphasize quality work. All encourage input at all levels. All are trying to get rid of fear and coercion.

This common agenda is also the agenda of the community. Businesses know they are in need of self-motivated problem-solvers in the workplace. Parents understand that threatening students with failure is not working. Educators know students and teachers are tired at the end of the day rather than re-energized. The common agenda is quality work, strong self-esteem, and responsible, thoughtful behavior.

Does this mean the visioning process is easy? That aligning practices flows effortlessly from the common vision? No, it does not. Consensus skills must be enhanced continually, and even then your organization may get stuck. This is predictable and it is manageable. The next stage of our journey will introduce you to some of our ideas about getting unstuck.

GETTING UNSTUCK

This chapter deals with transforming conflict from a negative concept to a positive one. When we embrace conflicts, we view them as a path to freedom. We have therefore chosen a character composed of three radicals, each of which represents a form of conflict. When the three kinds of conflict are put together and cannot escape until they achieve "oneness," the resulting character means liberation and freedom. When we closely examine freedom that is earned or costly, we will always find countless conflicts and strife in its evolution. Looking forward to the liberation gives us the strength and determination to keep on hammering at the conflicts until they are resolved.

GETTING UNSTUCK

Getting stuck is part of the change process. Out of chaos comes new form. "It is always darkest before the dawn" is a familiar saying. If you can't envision the dawn beyond the darkness, you may not have the tools to steer through this difficult period. You simply visualize yourself swiftly moving toward the rapids of destruction.

If you feel you have been adrift without a paddle, or rowing in a circle with one oar, or endlessly up and down the same channel, this is normal and help is at hand. We propose this book as a life preserver thrown from the shore. If you keep your head above water with your understanding of control theory, you can float about, get your bearings, and take notice of the many lifelines along the shore. Grab on to one you think will help. Nothing we propose will hurt you. One of these lifelines is also a guideline to help you navigate the rapids of change.

In this section we will revisit and elaborate on control theory concepts to help you keep moving forward. Review the information about the three types of organizational culture and share it with your staff, so they can assess where they are as a group and identify what their issues will be as they move from traditional to collegial relationships.

Review the information on conflict-resolution strategies and share it with your staff. If they can identify their personal strategies and commit to collaboration, the dynamics in your group will shift dramatically. This will be especially true if members publish to the group how they wish to change, so that the group can support them.

Learn the strategy for collapsing conflict. The third chapter in this section presents scenarios where staff collapse conflicts by identifying the needs behind each want and then together creating a new picture that meets all parties' needs. This control theory tool, introduced earlier at moving from want to need and in the Take Control Chart, is elaborated here as a specific technique for getting unstuck.

Conflict will begin to arise as a companion to implementation. As changes are initiated and staff begin to manage the consequences of change, it is predictable that there will be conflicting needs within the organization. If this conflict is not managed effectively, people may become discouraged and abandon the process.

Teaching the implementation dip will buy a bit of time, but the conflict will only be resolved with skill. These skills will be available to your team if they have been presented as part of the training package and if you model them. They are available in previous chapters of this book. They are brought to bear here as means of getting unstuck.

Do not be afraid of conflict. Realize that conflict is a necessary part of shifting from a congenial to a collegial organization. Create the conditions for your team to resolve conflict collaboratively.

COLLEGIAL CULTURE

In a quality organization, there is a collegial culture of expectations and relationships, which begins to develop through the learning of control theory and the dialogue of vision-setting. As you prepare to bring your practices into alignment with your wants, needs, beliefs, and values, this culture may merit specific attention.

In *Renewing America's Schools*, Carl Glickman observes that there are generally three positions a school can take along a cultural continuum. He classifies schools into three types: conventional, congenial, and collegial.

The Conventional School. This school is traditional. It is viewed mainly as a place to work. Teachers tend to operate autonomously. They close their doors and do their jobs. They tend to be somewhat competitive with each other.

The Congenial School. In this school friendship is as important as work. It is known as a social school where everyone gets along very well. Birthdays are always remembered.

This school, because belonging is so important, tends to be somewhat conflict-averse. When a difficult discusssion arises in a staff meeting, silence descends or the issue is dropped. Although vigorous dialogue is absent in staff meetings, gossip abounds in small groups.

Scott Peck calls this pseudocommunity.

> The basic assumption of pseduocommunity is that the problem of individual differences should be avoided....A way in which this occurs is the proposal to split into subgroups. This proposal is particularly seductive because of the prevailing false dogma that fifteen or so is the ideal maximum group size. But in my experience it is invariably an attempt to flee from the group as a whole and its task of building itself into a genuine community.
>
> *The Different Drum, p.109-110*

The Collegial School. This school is not afraid of vigorous dialogue. It is characterized by the satisfaction derived from professional interactions. Fundamental work is being done to examine educational practices in the light of beliefs and best knowledge. There is no fear of disagreement. Staff do not fear paradigm shifts or the big questions that change lives. They maintain their belonging and deepen it through sharing ideals and differences.

It is hard to shift from congenial to collegial, because people fear they will have to sacrifice their caring for each other, and conflict naturally exaggerates this fear. Staff can make this shift, however, with teaching and support for collaboration.

One way to promote this is to explore with staff the difference between a superficial conversation and a quality conversation with a friend. Have them evaluate which way they want to talk with each other. It may also be helpful to have staff explore the differences between their discussion mode and their dialogue mode. It is important for you to frame vigorous dialogue as a growth opportunity: to understand another's point of view is true learning.

School Example:

Judy's Story of the Shift From Congenial to Collegial

My first assignment as a new principal was at a congenial school. The director told me, "This school has always had a reputation in the district for being a place where everyone gets along, everyone is happy and cares about each other." Then he added, "Just don't blow it!"

As a first-year principal, I enjoyed the congenial spirit of the school. It was a fun place to be. Staff welcomed me with warmth and friendliness. They told me, "This is such a great school. People are good friends. Everyone really cares about each other and gets along."

The social committee was an active group, planning social gatherings throughout the year. Several other committees organized school-wide projects and events to build school spirit. Staff birthdays were celebrated. Every day in December a different group provided treats. Most people met in the staff lounge each morning to have coffee and visit before school started. Everyone met again to eat lunch together. The same small groups ate at the same table each day. These same groups sat together at faculty meetings.

The word "fair" surfaced frequently when people expressed different options or solutions to problems.

Fairness was defined as equality. If one class wanted to go on a field trip, everyone had to go or no one could go. If one teacher requested a set of material, every other teacher wanted the same material or the same amount of money to order something else.

At faculty meetings, a few individuals dominated the discussions. When feelings of anger or resentment surfaced, the group became withdrawn and quiet. The nonverbal signals were visible: downcast eyes, darting glances, crossed arms, squirming, stiffness, tears. At this point, the topic would be dropped if possible.

The usual strategy to settle differences of opinion was voting. The voting followed little discussion for fear of people's feelings being hurt. Another strategy was forming a small committee to address the problems and decide for the group. A common statement about a committee's decision for the group was, "Don't complain about the decision, because everyone had a chance to serve on the committee. If you don't like the decision, next time be on the committee." In other words, you waived your rights when you didn't choose to volunteer.

Discontent and complaints were raised in small groups after the meeting. Rather than expressing feelings and thoughts directly to those with conflicting perspectives, people with similar beliefs, philosophies, and pictures would gossip about those who had different pictures. Many times the facts were distorted and not even true. Instead of problems getting solved, conflicts intensified and became more complicated.

Some individuals would withdraw and say, "I'm just going to my classroom, do my own thing, and not worry about anybody else." They appeared resigned to being offended. They were very quiet at most faculty meetings, but occasionally they would display outbursts of anger regarding particular topics. Sometimes they would even walk out of faculty meetings.

Other people were accommodating. They seemed happy and would say, "Things aren't so bad. We really think the same way. Our thinking is not that different."

Some people would compete with others. They had an intense need for power. They wanted to know what others were doing, using, and purchasing, so they could do, use, and purchase at least the same and preferably better things.

Conflict was avoided at any cost in this congenial faculty. To avoid conflict, people would even intentionally say the opposite of how they thought and felt in a meeting. Although people were hurt and resentful underneath, the most important thing was getting along on the surface.

For example, at a formal grade-level meeting, a group of teachers unanimously agreed on certain procedures for a school activity. Later that day all of the teachers except one asked to meet privately in my office. They said they had all agreed at the meeting because they wanted to keep harmony, but now they wanted me to know what they were really thinking. They told me it was difficult for them to disagree with the other person at their grade level because they feared she would get very angry and not want to work together with them. They said, "It's easier to just agree with her so we can all get along."

Then they expressed a very different picture of how they wanted the activity to be conducted. They also asked me to take action on their private requests instead of following the decisions reached at their open grade-level meeting. Of course, they didn't want me to mention our private meeting.

Peter Senge refers to this phenomenon when he describes the "smooth surface" team:

> In the "smooth surface" teams, members believe that they must suppress their conflicting views in order to maintain the team—if each person spoke her or his mind, the team would be torn apart by irreconcilable differences.
>
> The Fifth Discipline, *p. 249*

Conflict is not valued in a congenial group, it is seen as a threat to the harmony of the group. It is important for people to be happy and friendly, even if it is just on the surface. Diversity is avoided. Differences of opinion are minimized or ignored for the sake of unity. But resentment and frustration break down the very trust and respect such groups try so earnestly to preserve. People use passive-aggressive behaviors to get what they want. Decisions are made behind the scenes, so people don't understand the decision-making process. Thus, surface congeniality is antithetical to quality. An organization must learn collegiality if it is to grow to quality.

Moving from a congenial to a collegial staff will not be easy. It is a gradual process. Several factors contribute to this shift, most significantly, learning control theory. As you move from a stimulus-response view of the world to a control theory view of the world, you will begin the transformation from a congenial group to a collegial group.

Control theory teaches that all of us develop "pictures" in our heads, and it is almost impossible for any two of us to have exactly the same picture in our heads at exactly the same moment. People invent, learn, relearn, and use negotiation behaviors. These ways of behaving help work out picture differences. With a control theory perspective, staff come to assume people will have different pictures. Instead of trying to convert others to have the same picture, the focus shifts to trying to understand other peoples' pictures.

As staff continue their dialogue about various control theory concepts like maximum degrees of freedom, unlimited resources, and win/win mentality, they realize the value of moving from congeniality to collegiality. Since you will not all travel this road at the same rate, the transition presents challenges.

Those who have made the shift to collegiality will value dialogue about different perspectives. They will consider this a sign of a healthy environment. They will view conflict as productive. Through dialogue they will reach creative solutions they could not have thought of alone.

Others will still find conflict stressful. They will become uncomfortable during discussions of different perspectives. They will take things personally and feelings will be hurt. In Judy's experience, this group wanted things to be the way they used to be—calm, peaceful, uniform, the same. They still wanted to take a vote and have everyone agree to do the same thing. They wished they could be one big happy family again! Their comments included: "Nobody comes to the staff lounge anymore. Nobody wants to be on the social committee anymore. We never do anything together anymore. Everybody is doing their own thing. Peoples' feelings are hurt. We're not like a happy family anymore."

All wanted unity, but there were different pictures of that. Some wanted to return to a more congenial spirit. Their picture of unity included having coffee and visiting together in the morning, everyone voting to do the same thing, more staff get-togethers, more school-wide activities, and focus on a family theme at school. Those who welcomed a more collegial spirit also wanted to focus on unity, but their picture of unity included diversity being valued, self-evaluation rather than being evaluated by others, differences of opinion welcomed, respect for individual differences, and maximum degrees of freedom.

The challenge for you at this point will be to go forward and not turn back. People may be looking for someone to blame in the midst of conflict, and the principal can be a common target. Rather than taking it personally and becoming defensive, it is important to understand that blaming is a natural part of the process. Instead of minimizing the differences and avoiding conflict, reaffirm your belief in the value of conflict.

> Contrary to popular myth, great teams are not characterized by an absence of conflict. On the contrary, in my experience, one of the most reliable indicators of a team that is continually learning is the visible conflict of ideas. In great teams, conflict becomes productive.

> On the other hand, in mediocre teams one of two conditions usually surround conflict. Either there is an appearance of no conflict on the surface, or there is rigid polarization.

The difference between great teams and mediocre teams lies in how they face conflict and deal with the defensiveness that invariably surrounds conflict.

Peter Senge, The Fifth Discipline, *p. 249*

In the midst of conflict, self-evaluate: Ask, "What am I thinking? What am I doing?" Here is a thinking/action plan we recommend.

Think:

Conflict is a normal part of the change process.

It's OK that we have different pictures of the value of conflict.

We're all doing our best to resolve conflicts, whether avoiding, accommodating, competing, compromising, or collaborating.

It's OK that some of us are having difficulty.

All behavior is purposeful.

What do they need to move forward?

How can I help them meet their need and still move forward?

Do:

Teach about the difference between congeniality and collegiality.

Teach about the styles of conflict resolution.

Review best knowledge about conflict.

Let staff do the work of resolving conflicts.

Ask questions to understand different pictures and needs.

SUMMARY

A Quality School enjoys a collegial culture of roles and relationships. Each individual member is valued and encouraged to contribute his or her own unique gifts and perspectives. There is sometimes conflict in a collegial environment, but this conflict is neither personalized nor avoided. It is accepted, even embraced, as an opportunity to discover better ways of working.

By recognizing and valuing individual differences, a quality organization spares itself blame, denial, rationalization, and scapegoating. The energy otherwise drained by conflict is directed creatively to learning and growing, developing better ways to meet common goals while meeting individual needs.

The transition to collegiality can be difficult, but it is indispensable, so learn to stay in thinking and action to keep your balance and promote change. Collaboration is worth the effort.

COLLABORATION

Collaboration occurs when everybody is controlling who they can—themselves—and contributing their best efforts to a solution while leaving others free to do likewise. There is no conflict here because collaboration transforms conflict.

The word conflict comes from the Latin "con," which means together, and "fligro," which means to dash or strike. This word embodies in it a harshness, combat and struggle. This coming together epitomizes the attempt of two entities to occupy the same space. It implies that one party must be displaced. The word conflict is filled with the sparks which come from the striking together of two parties. These sparks can energize the creation of quality, taking the organization to new heights of creativity and effectiveness if there is a common vision and if collaboration is sought.

The visioning process described in Moving Forward rests upon consensus, seeking and clarifying the overlap of quality world pictures, so that people "feel together" and want to make social contracts. Consensus emphasizes the common ground that already exists.

Collaboration, for transforming conflict and getting unstuck, is a different process. It is essential for making plans to act on beliefs. Collaboration is the process used to create **new** common ground among people.

It is more toward confluence, which comes from the Latin words "con" *(with)* and "fluo" *(to flow)*. Confluence occurs when two bodies, such as two rivers, flow together. One does not subsume the other or conquer the other. Each contributes its essence to the whole. Collaboration seeks to create conditions for confluence rather than for conflict.

Collaboration is the art of win/win negotiation, where each party gets what it needs by creating new options. Collaboration is used when the parties first believe that, "If you get what you want, I won't get what I want." Initially there is strong potential for adversity, and the sparks of conflict threaten to flame out of control.

This is signaled by people saying "Yes, but..." or "That won't work." It is manifested by the behaviors of competition, avoidance, and sometimes accommodation. Here are some things people will be saying and doing to indicate that collaboration is not happening.

Collaboration Is Not Happening When:

1. Voices are loud—not just excited but angry.

2. People say, "I disagree."

3. People say, "You're wrong."

4. People say, "You don't understand."

5. People withdraw.

6. People say, "That's fine," in a not-fine tone.

7. People say, "I don't care" or "Whatever."

8. People bring up past problem situations.

Have you encountered these behaviors? Where do they lead? Where do they come from? They are the legacies of the stimulus-response orientation, the belief that either you control others or they control you. Not wishing to be controlled because of their inbuilt need for freedom, people seek the power to control others to assure independence from them. They assume it is a dog-eat-dog world, and of course the lesser of the two evils is to be the eater.

Control theory, on the other hand, teaches that in the long term you can only control yourself. Only by superior force applied twenty-four hours a day can one person control another. War experiences worldwide in recent years show that the moment the force is withdrawn, people go back to being the way they want to be.

Control theory teaches win/win solutions rather than trying to conquer others. In a conflict situation, this translates into seeking solutions that are mutually need-satisfying.

Another legacy of stimulus-response thinking is the belief that there are limited resources. If you accept the belief that resources, and therefore options, are finite, you naturally are strongly predisposed to put your own interests first for the sake of survival. The result is competitive behavior, and this leads directly into conflict in the struggle to control others to maintain ownership of these limited resources.

Control theory also teaches that the concept of limited resources is open to challenge. Resources are only as limited as creativity. Collaborative creative thinking can result in the discovery of resources which were not previously obvious. To get this kind of thinking, you need the confluence of differing perceptions which may initially appear mutually exclusive or conflicting.

How do you know when collaboration is happening?

Collaboration Is Happening When:

1. Consideration and courage are in balance.

2. Respect is demonstrated by listening, questioning, paraphrasing, acknowledging, and clarifying.

3. There is nodding, smiling, sitting in proximity.

4. People make such statements as, "Let's put your idea and my idea together."

5. People are looking for similarities, "What do we agree on?"

6. Everyone is satisfied. They say so and they look so.

Are these the behaviors you want to be seeing? Will this increase the serenity and productivity of your organization? To get to collaboration, it is helpful to study with your team the styles of conflict resolution.

STYLES OF CONFLICT RESOLUTION

There are five identifiable roles one can adopt when faced with a potential conflict situation. These roles are avoidance, accommodation, competition, compromise, and collaboration. Each of these styles of conflict resolution has a different position with regard to the win/lose axis.

Avoidance of a conflict, or withdrawal, is really a lose/lose situation. One loses the opportunity to influence the group, and the group loses the value of those ideas. Mind you, one can wisely withdraw from a situation if the issue under discussion has no importance.

Accommodation means one accepts not having personal needs met in favor of others meeting their needs. This is usually a lose/win position because it is a loss for the person who accommodates and a win for those who benefit from the concession.

Competition is a win/lose style. The winners use their personal resources to overpower the needs of the losers. It appears to be a win for the victors, but the losers will have frustration. This frustration will reduce energy and increase resistance to moving in the direction won by the victors.

Compromise is a half-win/half-lose position. Compromise means cutting one's losses by bartering away part of what one wants. It can only produce short-term relief. Compromise means doing it his way half the time and her way half the time, or dividing up the resources so each gets half. Though this model appears to work, it guarantees that at least half the time somebody's needs are not getting met. This mismatch of needs and resources results in frustration.

Collaboration is a win/win situation for both parties. In order to get collaboration, both parties must work to expand resources for a solution that is mutually agreeable.

Covey sees these various styles as a function of the degree and balance of courage and consideration—courage of one's own convictions, consideration for the convictions of others.

Figure 12. **Conflict-Resolution Styles**

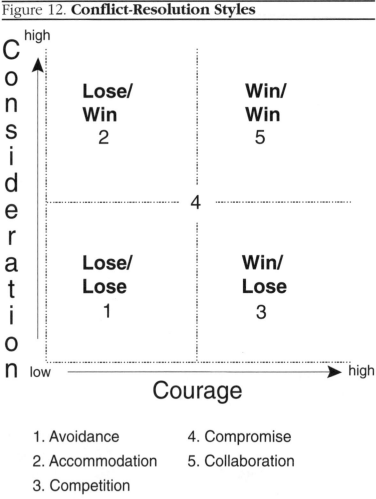

1. Avoidance 4. Compromise
2. Accommodation 5. Collaboration
3. Competition

Stephen Covey, The Seven Habits of Highly Effective People, *p. 218*

Changing Your Style

It is useful to take staff through the process of first self-analyzing personal styles and then seeking to understand how their styles have worked. It is important to validate that whatever has been done is not bad, before asking everybody to self-evaluate to see if they could do better.

An indispensable part of this process is for you to coach and model the self-assessment of individual conflict-resolution preferences. Such modeling might go like this.

> Whatever I'm choosing to do is better than something else I might be doing. All behavior is purposeful. The behavior I don't like in myself is meeting a need or I wouldn't be doing it. If I avoid conflict, what could be worse? Probably being attacked. If I am overly aggressive, what could be worse? Possibly not caring about what is at stake. If I am too accommodating, what need is being met? Is it my belonging need with this group? When I compromise, I am avoiding losing everything by losing only half. When I refuse to compromise, I either believe I can win or I have decided to give up caring about the issue. When I understand my personal style of conflict resolution, I can see where I might change to get more balance.

The next step in the process is to declare a desire to experiment with a different style by either being more courageous or more considerate, to ask for support from colleagues, and to try the new plan for a period of time.

After this you can self-evaluate again to see if the new plan is getting more of what you want.

For example, one director of programs decided he was being too accommodating. As a result, his supervisor was having to attend his meetings whenever decisions were to be made. When the director published to the working team his desire to be more courageous, his supervisor agreed to more considerate by staying out of the meetings so the director could pace up. They mutually decided on a suitable time frame for the experiment.

Understanding that the goal of this process is to increase courage and/or consideration for greater collaboration, it is also essential that the plan take account of the need or offer protection of the value that the original strategy met. For example, if withdrawing was protecting financial security, the person needs to hear from you that asserting will not jeopardize the job.

Win/Win Conflict Resolution

Always approach a potential conflict in a non-adversarial way. View it as a conflict of needs, not necessarily of persons. The solution sought will be one in which both parties can meet their needs. Herb Cohen says,

> If the focus shifts from defeating each other to defeating the problem, everyone can benefit. In a collaborative Win-Win negotiation we are trying to produce an outcome that provides acceptable gain to all parties. Conflict is regarded as a natural part of the human condition. If conflict is viewed as a problem to be solved, creative solutions can be found that enhance the positions of both sides, and the parties may even be brought closer together.
>
> You Can Negotiate Anything, *p.150*

He also cautions against viewing the pie to be shared as a fixed quantity.

> We should see our true interests as complementary and in effect ask each other, "How can we get together in a way that will make the total pie bigger, so there's more to go around?"...A negotiation is more than an exchange of material objects. It is a way of acting and behaving that can develop understanding, belief, acceptance, respect, and trust.
>
> You Can Negotiate Anything, *p.154.*

Seek always to understand the person's needs and point of view as well as your own. Clarify for yourself what you want. Understand the values behind what you want and the need that will be met for you by getting what you want. Remember to seek to get your need met even if you can't get your specific want.

In order to understand collaboration, it is important to explore the control theory concept of degrees of freedom. From a mathematical point of view there are limited degrees of freedom in any equation of human behavior. If you wish to understand this better, read William Powers' article "Degrees of Freedom in Social Interactions."

We introduced the concept of degrees of freedom in Getting Started. We revisit it here to summarize some of Power's points that are germane to our understanding of how to deal with conflict.

1. The more degrees of freedom you have, the more opportunities you have to achieve what you want and to meet your needs.

2. Because you have a social need to operate in harmony with others (belonging), you work

with them to establish common expectations, beliefs, and goals. This simplifies your interactions with each other, you can commit to each other, you can predict how others will behave based on these commitments, and you can build trust based on this predictability.

3. The more homogeneous a society becomes, the fewer options there are for individual expression. The freedom need is disrupted as options decrease.

4. There is danger of moving into conflict if there are not enough options for all to meet their needs. Conflict means trying to have power over others.

Maximizing degrees of freedom—a control theory practice strategy—therefore becomes the goal of collaboration. Using skills you already have begun to develop, you can guide and support collaboration through the following processes to avert or resolve potential conflict situations.

1. Move from the specific wants to identify the general needs of both (all) parties.

2. Explore the common ground of both (all) parties.

3. Frame up and develop a direction for the solution which includes the expressed needs of both (all) parties. This frame-up is the position from which the parties can begin to design back to a solution.

4. Lead a brainstorming of all possible variables for change. These could include clarifying perceptions of what titles mean, redefining roles so that both (all) parties can better meet their needs, reviewing timelines to find more flexibility, and creating new options.

5. Seek best knowledge with regard to the options brainstormed.

6. Adopt a plan and develop a strategy.

Losing to Gain

Losing to gain is a special case of win/win conflict resolution. It requires a clear vision, personal courage, and trust in the developmental process. It is always a negotiating option, but it may have special relevance for you during the transition to collegiality.

When an organization is attempting to move from a traditional boss system toward lead management, there will always be a point at which the power of authority is challenged to see if leaders are serious about sharing responsibility and power. It is difficult to predict when this challenge will occur. It may occur between teacher and students, principal and staff, or supervisor and staff. Sometimes this challenge is delayed and surfaces in an issue which has the potential to damage the system. Such an example was one Canadian school district where the challenge from staff to management came to the bargaining table and resulted in a six-week job action. Share power early on in the process to avoid a disastrous outcome.

An example of losing to gain is given in the article "Detours on the Road to Site-Based Management." Staff challenged the wisdom of the principal who questioned their plan to have detailed notes from each of several core team meetings typed up by the secretary. He felt it would be unwieldy. The staff prevailed because they felt, in the shared decision-making process, that such transactions were important to record.

After the second day of this experiment, staff came to the principal indicating that the information generated was too extensive to record; they asked that the plan be abandoned. The principal refused to change the plan without them reconvening staff. This was done promptly and the plan revised.

This is an example of losing to gain, or win/win. The principal "lost" the first round but "won" because he demonstrated willingness to let staff improvise. He then won a second time when he refused to accept responsibility for solving the problem which ensued. The staff won because they had the courage to try something new. They won a second time when they reconvened the group promptly to solve the problem. Both parties maintained a win/win focus by avoiding criticism and staying so win-oriented. And the organization won when the principal modeled and the staff experienced losing-to-gain.

The organization, in its growth to collegial culture, always wins—and so do its individual members—whenever conflict-resolution skill increases through application. Confidence in one's own and others' courage and consideration is a direct result of successful experience in an environment that values both. To give your staff this kind of successful learning experience, try the collaboration process described below.

COLLABORATION PROCESS

Move in the direction of collaboration through a five-step process of conflict resolution. This can be a thirty-minute process that combines several control theory strategies: (1) group-evaluate, (2) self-evaluate, (3) collapse the conflict, (4) brainstorm options, (5) create the plan.

1. **Group-Evaluate with Cross-Checking Questions.** Have the parties "group-evaluate," or in some cases "couple-evaluate," the road they are on in their interaction by asking cross-checking questions:

    Is this going the way we want it to go?

    If we keep on this way will it get better?

    Could it get worse?

    Would that be satisfactory to you/us?"

    This group evaluation creates the first common ground.

2. **Self-Evaluate with the Take Control Chart.** Ask each person to self-evaluate using the Take Control Chart. Have them identify what they don't want, what they do want, and their need. They may choose to self-restitute at this time. (The Restitution Triangle can be useful for a person who has difficulty self-evaluating.)

3. **Collapse the Conflict.** Use the Collapse the Conflict Chart to bring out each party's need and frame up a direction for a solution that takes into consideration each person's need. It is crucial to avoid any blame or fault.

4. **Brainstorm Options.** Have the parties together create solutions that meet both or all parties' needs. Each person offers what they think they are willing to contribute to the solution.

5. **Create the Plan.** The best plans result when as many people as possible offer to do something toward a solution. This will go very quickly if no one feels coerced. Individuals will speak for themselves, saying, "I would be willing to...." As the group gets more skilled, the process goes more easily.

As an example of how efficient this strategy can be, Diane recalls the following experience.

> In December 1976 I was doing training at an Indian Band controlled school. There were 120 staff. The first morning the question arose, "Can we smoke?" I turned the question over to the group, asking what was their protocol. One person spoke up and said, "It's a racist issue. Everyone knows the Indians are the smokers." Ten minutes into the workshop and we were on the verge of conflict. It increased as people began "gunnysacking" each other, until I asked the group, "Is this how you want to be spending your time with me? If we keep on this way will it be productive?" They said "No."

Figure 13. **Collapse the Conflict Chart**

For two people:

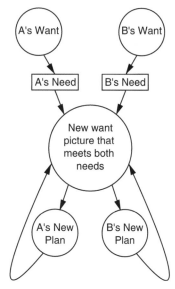

For a group:

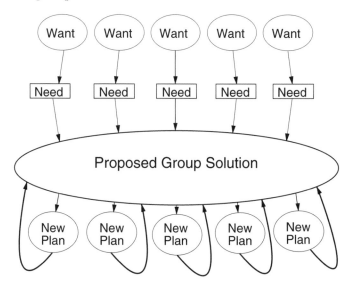

I summarized the needs expressed, not the problem. "What I hear is some people are concerned about the health hazard of so much smoke in a room of 120 people. Others of you need freedom to meet your needs. You all agree that the conflict is not giving the group a good feeling. Some people feel they have no control here. You've all heard what has been said. I ask each of you individually to try as best you can to be part of the solution instead of part of the problem. We'll evaluate at lunch time.

At lunch the group evaluated, and one person said "While we were having the discussion, I counted forty-eight cigarettes smoked. After you asked us to help, three cigarettes were smoked. People do want to do better."

People do not need to agree on a single answer. Individuals control themselves to make their own unique contributions to a solution.

School Example:

Collaboration to Create a Complex Solution

At a magnet school in North Carolina, Diane facilitated a collaboration process to help the group create a complex solution to a potentially difficult problem. The questioned procedure at this school was mass movement of the entire student body three times a day, during which teachers were expected to stand in their doorways for monitoring.

There was some feeling that this was not working, and this concern became apparent when there began to be complaints that some of the teachers were doing more monitoring than others. Rather than sinking into blaming and resistance, the group agreed to seek a collaborative solution. Here is the way their group- and self-evaluations came together along the Take Control Chart.

Figure 14. **Take Control Chart**

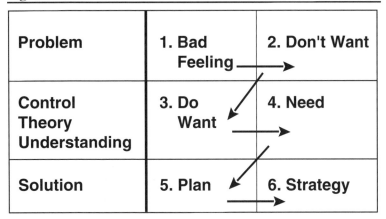

Problem	1. Bad Feeling	2. Don't Want
Control Theory Understanding	3. Do Want	4. Need
Solution	5. Plan	6. Strategy

1. Bad Feeling. There was acknowledgment by the whole group that something wasn't right about this procedure. Staff dissatisfaction was visible and increasing.

2. Don't Want. Staff were very concerned lest children be at risk for injury during rapid, rowdy movement through congested corridors. They also feared that inadequate supervision might compromise the safety of some students with special needs. Some teachers felt their professional duty of teaching was sacrificed to the policing assignment. Others were frustrated by lost teaching time when classes started late. There was a tendency for some teachers to think of their colleagues as shirkers for too-lax surveillance or enforcers for too-rigid monitoring. Clearly, the problem here was complex.

3. Do Want. Together staff identified the conditions they wanted to meet and the underlying needs. Some staff stated a desire for more control, others wanted more freedom to be preparing for their classes during the transition periods. All wanted to protect their camaraderie and their good opinions of one another. Everyone wanted minimal risk to children's safety. The principal wanted students to like school, all affirmed a desire to help students move towards self-discipline.

4. Need. It turned out that this particular procedure was one which had impact on all the needs—belonging, power, fun, freedom, and survival—of students, and on the staff's needs especially for belonging, power, and freedom. The current plan was not providing for all these needs, and everyone was willing to revise it.

5. Plan. To figure out exactly what should change, the group decided to seek information. At the next change, thirty staff dispersed discreetly around the school to find the facts about the concerns identified. Here is the result of this search for best knowledge.

1. There was a danger spot at one intersection where a brick wall could be the scene of an accident.

2. Students moving in a crowd spontaneously opened their ranks to create access for a student on crutches.

3. Less than one percent of students were late to class.

4. No one got hurt.

5.   A boy in time out came from the office to greet the wave of passing students, thus interrupting his planning time.

6.   Some teachers were at their doorways, others weren't.

7.   Children were happy, enjoying the movement, not fighting.

The observers were satisfied that their research was representative of the thrice-daily activity and narrowed the range of concerns their strategy should address. Best knowledge revealed some of their concerns to be without factual basis and focused attention on the others.

6. Strategy. Diane invited the group to begin creating solutions, saying, "I invite each of you as an individual to think about what you can do to become part of the solution, so we can improve this situation so that teachers have some freedom to prepare, students can socialize as they move, your administration feels there is adequate control and accountability, we keep a good feeling among ourselves, and we uphold safety. What do you suggest?"

Individuals at this time were anxious to contribute. The list of contributors grew. One person said, "I've been one of the slackers and I'm willing to get to my door during movement." The principal said, "I'd like to be on a committee to look at how we could schedule so staff don't have to be on call every movement period."

The custodians agreed to check the brick wall. The time-out option was going to be tightened for the young man who was rewarded by being out of class. Several teachers volunteered to review the beliefs with their classes, focusing on movement in the halls. One teacher said, "I think I've been too rigid in my expectations of my colleagues. I've decided to evaluate myself rather than evaluate others. I think I'll be happier."

As individuals contributed, a feeling of empowerment swept through the group. What had been discouragement and potential adversity had evolved into hope and helpfulness. Staff began to understand that self-evaluating, collecting best knowledge, and creating individual solutions for group problems was an exciting and need-fulfilling activity. They closed the session with the comment, "And we can get faster at doing this!"

SUMMARY

In collaboration, seek to combine the perspectives, ideas, and solutions of all parties into win/win strategies so that everyone's needs can be met. Collaboration develops acceptance, respect, and new resources, leaving the organization and its individual members stronger. Understanding this will create conditions for yourself and others to learn more collaborative conflict-resolution styles through increasing courage and consideration with constant attention to the needs which underlie differing want pictures.

COLLAPSING CONFLICT

The strategy for collapsing conflict is a specific control theory contribution to the theory and process of collaboration. Though we have mentioned it in previous chapters, we believe it is worthy of further elaboration. This chapter therefore presents scenarios where staff collapse conflicts by identifying the needs behind their wants and then together creating a new picture which meets all parties' needs.

Everyone is born conflicted in basic needs and therefore builds pictures into quality world albums that are in conflict with each other. Is there anyone who has not been in conflict? When working with people in conflict, you can help by asking the person first to identify whether the conflict is internal—intrapersonal—or with another person—interpersonal.

Intrapersonal conflict can be resolved by asking oneself the reality therapy questions, *What do I want?* and *What do I think my need is?* The answer might be, "I want to finish my degree and my need is power."

The next two questions elicit the competing need: *What is standing between me and what I say I want? What am I doing instead of what I want?* The answers to these questions will pull out the need one is meeting when not working on the degree. Often the answer will be "just about anything else," which could lead to the freedom need; or it might be "spending time with my family," which would target the belonging need; or it could be "dancing and partying," which would point to the fun need.

Whatever is standing between you and what you want is your perceived competing need. All behavior is purposeful. Even procrastination is meeting a need. We say "perceived" competing need because true conflict arises only when no behavior can be found to meet both needs.

Help staff frame up perceived conflicts by asking them to figure out how to get both needs met rather than choosing between them. Learn and teach saying **and** instead of **or**.

For example, you want to go out on Friday and socialize with staff (fun), but you have to do your grading (power). Instead of thinking, "Choose one," learn to ask, "If you could do both, would it get you what you want?" Now grading papers in the lounge is probably not the most effective combination, but perhaps you can create a way to have fun and get the job done.

If you can learn to identify the two needs and create a way to get both, you are less likely to become burnt out or disgruntled. Have each friend grade a paper? Perhaps. Have fun tomorrow? Maybe. Take the students out for a soda and have them self-evaluate? Is that your picture? The options are endless. Your brain will keep generating them. Your job is to self-evaluate, "Is what I'm choosing getting all my needs met?"

CONFLICT OUTCOMES

Often conflict is not only intrapersonal but also inter-personal. What one person wants seems to violate another person's need. In this case, you can help identify the need and then see whether another want picture can be developed which will not be in conflict with others. If this is not successful, negotiation may generate ideas for both parties to get what they need. Remember, this may not be what they originally wanted.

If one person wins, you will have created a competitive situation. If one person gives in, you will have accommodation. If the conflict is ignored, you will have avoidance. If there is a trade-off, you will have compromise. Only if both parties get their needs met will you have collaboration.

Let's look at a social example. Diane went with her husband to a wedding dance. They were sitting at a table with some of her unmarried friends who were without escorts. Her husband is a good dancer, but he chose to dance only with her. At first she enjoyed herself dancing. After a while, however, she began to experience some frustration, and then she wanted to control his behavior. She needed to analyze her own behavior in order to generate some options for herself.

This meant she had to identify where her conflict lay. She realized she felt responsible for her friends having a good time (belonging). But this desire had the potential to lead to trouble if she attempted to coerce her partner (power) to dance with her single friends.

What were her choices?

1. She could explain her conflict to him and hope he would choose to dance with them, at the same time saying, "It's up to him."

2. She could try to shift her perception so she did not feel so responsible for her friends having a good time.

3. She could take action by asking some single male friends to join their table and thereby provide options for dancing.

4. She could explain how she felt to her friends so they'd know she wasn't oblivious to their needs.

5. She could decide to go home early, thereby resolving her perceived conflict.

Less desirable solutions would be: (6) guilting her partner, (7) withdrawing her affection, (8) fighting with him, (9) getting drunk, (10) refusing to dance.

Of the ten possible solutions, each would be somewhat need-fulfilling. The reason the first five are more desirable is that they have the potential to resolve the conflict for her without disrupting her other needs or those of another person.

Of the desirable choices, the one over which she has the most control is the choice to shift her perception to take herself out of conflict. Perceiving her partner as deliberately wanting to hurt her friends or herself is guaranteed to exacerbate her conflict. He is just meeting his need. (As a matter of fact, he later said he had been shy.)

Whatever the choice may be, it appears that there is a winner in each case, but you might think about the fact that there is a cost to every victory. The reason for this is that when people's needs are disrupted by being in the one-down position, they will attempt to right the imbalance. How they do this may cost the victor. In this example, Diane may get her way but she may lose belonging from her husband or other friends. Truly there never is a clear-cut winner unless everyone wins.

Figure 15. **Conflict-Resolution Outcomes**

SOLUTION	Win/Lose	Lose/Win	Lose/Lose	Half-Win/Half-Lose	Win/Win
She guilts him into what she wants.	She wins. He loses.				
She dances and leaves her friends.		She loses. He wins.			
Both sit there.			He loses. She loses.		
He takes turns dancing with her and her friends.				He half-wins. She half-wins.	
Create new resources.					He wins. She wins.

The win/win option for resolving conflict is to create new resources so everyone's needs can be met. In the example used here, creating new resources might include finding some other partners for the friends, dancing as a group, going to a club to dance, changing their picture so women choose to dance together, or discussing with friends and finding they don't even want to dance with him!

As you review these examples, you become aware that there is almost always conflict whenever you are attempting to control another. If you do this, it automatically results in the other person experiencing a desire to be free from you. A better way to deal with this is to tell the other person what you need and ask for their help in whatever way they wish to give it.

Working to collapse the conflict in win/win solutions between management and staff is always desirable. One example which comes to mind is a situation which arose in a corrections facility. The guards were requesting a higher level of security at the facility. It was a hot issue, since implementing what they requested would cost thousands of dollars. Staff were threatening to strike.

In facilitating the meeting, the mediation team asked the reality therapy cross-checking questions, since what the guards wanted fell into the category of unattainable requests.

Why is it important to you?

Then we would feel safe.

How would it be better for you?

We wouldn't have to be tensed up on guard and watch our backs at all times.

What would you have that you don't have now?

We'd have a response to our demands.

What would that mean to you?

It would mean management cared.

As facilitators, it was then our job to frame up all their responses to create the parameters for a possible solution. This frame-up sounded something like this: "If management could demonstrate concern for staff, by working with you to create a safer environment, so you didn't have to watch your backs all the time, would it be going in the right direction? They can't at this time approve the expenditure you request, but your safety is important to them, and how you feel about your job is an important aspect of dynamic security."

This initiative temporarily defused the adversarial situation. Now the guards were ready to seek a collaborative solution. Real change came about as a result of further discussion with management, which generated specific new attainable want pictures: meetings with the inmate committee to get their suggestions for providing a safe environment for all persons in the area at night, new scheduling to provide more frequent opportunities for upper management to show interest in the new projects being initiated at each unit level. None of this cost more money, but each of these addressed the staff's deep needs that previously had been manifest in dogmatic demands for more locks. That several levels of the organization shared in the solution made it a jointly owned process.

CONFLICT LEGACIES

Learn to collapse potential conflicts by presenting options which take into consideration both the needs of the person and the needs of the system. Collaborate not only through compromise but through a process whereby all parties get what they need. Too often in compromise, both parties get half of what they need or get what they need half the time. That means everybody is in pain half of the time.

Figure 16. **Legacies of Conflict**		
LOSE-LOSE	COMPROMISE	WIN-WIN
Winner loses belonging, loser gets even: both lose.	Both get what they need half the time.	Creative solution: both meet needs, relationship grows stronger,
Both give up, everybody loses.	Both get half what they need. Opportunity lost.	new resources are created.

You will notice that in summarizing the legacies of conflict, we used only three categories: lose/lose, compromise, and win/win. It is customary in such discussions to use other categories for win/lose and lose/win, and our previous review of conflict-resolution styles might suggest that such categories exist.

It is our experience, however, that while this may be true for individuals, it does not apply to a quality organization. When two members of a team are in conflict, we find it simply is not possible for one to win unless both do. Defeat of an individual team member costs the team that member's energy (lost to "failure"), commitment, and effort. Worse, it weakens the team by disrupting the relationship between "victor" and "victim."

We therefore believe that the strategies of avoidance, accommodation, withdrawal, and competition all result in net losses to the quality organization. Avoidance—evading or ignoring conflict—is movement away from collegiality back to the congenial environment where energy is diverted to surface smoothness instead of being available for problem-solving. Withdrawal represents giving up rather than following through on what could have been a productive dialogue. Accommodation likewise represents a lost opportunity to create new resources or discover new options.

Both withdrawal and accommodation also impair relationships. These "resolutions" may allow frustration to simmer and accumulate, eroding individual commitment and team strength. At best, accommodation and withdrawal are lost opportunities for deeper involvement and better solutions.

Competition likewise carries opportunity costs: individual efforts are in opposition when they might have created synergy. This style also has perhaps the highest risk for destroying teams if the loser's case goes underground or escalates in other forms.

It is our belief, therefore, that there are three legacies of conflict: (1) everybody loses, both individuals and organization; (2) everybody wins something, and the organization suffers no harm; or (3) a solution is created which meets everyone's needs and adds new strength to the team. Collapsing the conflict is always the strategy of choice.

School Example:

Judy Collapses a Conflict

Our staff had mixed concerns about moving from a self-contained classroom structure to a multi-age setting. Staff were at very different developmental stages regarding the implementation of multi-age grouping. Even though a variety of research, articles, and best knowledge on the topic was provided in the lounge for staff to read, some were not interested in reading the material. Staff also knew that only those who wanted to shift to multi-age grouping would be doing so.

Initially it was very difficult for the faculty to discuss this topic. Many staff were spinning on their back wheels. The technique we used to help us get started was design back. We talked about where we wanted to be at the end of our discussions, then identified what we needed to do to get there. We asked ourselves, "At our last faculty meeting on multi-age grouping, what will we know that we don't know now? What will we be saying to each other at that last meeting? What will we be doing to support the people who want to try multi-age grouping?"

This helped, because prior to this discussion people were focused on all the suspected problems of multi-age grouping. The list was long, but these problems changed from negatives to positives when we identified them as things we would know or have reached consensus on by our last meeting—scheduling with the specialists, managing mixed grades in the lunchroom and on the playground, handling parent requests, placing students with the next year's teacher, coordinating with Special Education, fostering unity among staff, expanding communication among staff, changing room assignments for staff, identifying teams, organizing all-school events, determining procedures for ordering supplies and materials for the next year.

Once we identified what we wanted to know at our last meeting, we planned how we would get there. We decided to meet each Thursday morning before school to discuss these issues and reach consensus on a plan of action. We wanted to gather and share information on multi-age grouping. We wanted to visit schools with multi-age grouping. We wanted to discuss these ideas with other educators.

At the end of this meeting most staff were looking forward to our weekly faculty meetings. We knew where we wanted to go and we had a plan to get there. We had designed back.

The enthusiasm for the weekly faculty meetings soon diminished, however, when unresolved conflict almost brought our progress to a halt. We experienced a common frustration with change. It was like a roller coaster ride, there were lots of ups and downs. After we took two steps forward, we would often take a step back.

At an inservice day, we had talked about what best knowledge says about multi-age grouping, and we had shared our personal visions with each other. We ended the meeting by setting the agenda for our next meeting to discuss the next important question: "If this is what we know and what we want, then what shall we do to move towards multi-age grouping?" It was a positive experience, and I assumed staff were ready to move forward.

But at a follow-up meeting, some staff expressed concern about going forward with multi-age grouping for the next year. There were comments like, "We need to slow down. We're moving too fast. We should read more about what the research says. Let's think more about this."

This phenomenon is sometimes called the implementation dip. Carl Glickman calls it the "hesitancy gap." He says many schools experience this when they move from the theory to the reality of implementation. He also warns that when you reach consensus on the ideal, the plan may break down in the details of personal change. One strategy to help create the conditions for staff to move forward at this critical juncture is to collapse the conflict by identifying the wants of various people or groups of people, understanding why it is important to them, identifying their needs, and then finding a win/win solution that is need-satisfying for all the parties.

Usually I would rather have staff identify the solution, but at times of great conflict, I will model for them how to identify the wants, validate the need, and create new common ground that is need-satisfying for all. After considerable reflection on this multi-age grouping issue, I shared my thoughts with staff and presented an option that took into consideration the needs of various teachers.

We have been having difficulty reaching consensus on how we want to move forward with multi-age grouping for next year. It feels like we are stalled. Let me summarize what I think I hear you saying.

Some of you are saying, "Let's not rush into this. Let's take more time to think about this. Let's spend next year reading, dialoguing, attending workshops, and visiting other schools."

This is important to you because you believe you're good at what you do. Your students' test scores are high. Your students are well-behaved. You like what you're doing. Why would you want to change something that isn't broken?

Others are saying, "I've been reading, visiting with others, and attending workshops on multi-age grouping. I'm ready to move forward, but not too fast. I'm not sure what multi-age grouping will look like in the end, but I want to start moving in that direction next year. I'm ready to take risks, I'm ready to learn from my mistakes. I don't want to wait for other staff before I move forward, but I'm willing to share with them any information I have gathered."

This is important to you because you want to be free to put into practice the new things you've learned. Some of you also want the support of your colleagues. You have shared your picture of what you want, and you want to be validated.

Is this what I hear you saying? Is this what you want?

If it is, I would like to suggest three key ideas for us to consider as we move forward: It's okay that people are at different stages. Flexibility is important if we are going to move forward. Proximity among cross-age teams is also important.

Based on this information, I am proposing for your consideration the following plan for next year. We keep our existing graded classroom structure, and we spend next year dialoguing, reading, visiting, and attending workshops. But we also support those who want to experiment with cross-age teaming, by providing flexibility in the schedule, and by arranging proximity between cross-age team members.

Throughout this kind of roller-coaster ride, there is a tendency for those who are uncomfortable to drop off and hence disrupt the process. For the process to unfold, it is important that involvement among participants remain strong.

School Example:

Judy Self-Evaluates Involvement

During a period when staff didn't appear to be getting along very well and conflicts continued unresolved, I remember a self-evaluation in which I asked myself, "What can I do differently to help staff reach more collaborative solutions?" I was aware that some staff were thinking and saying to each other things like, "I'm not in the principal's quality world, so you ask her because you are." This was not the kind of principal I wanted to be.

If I believe all staff have influence, then I want to create the conditions where all staff feel free to come to me and talk about what's important to them, knowing that I will not only listen but that I will value what they say, I will reflect on it, and as a result of their influence I will change my picture of the issue or situation. If this is what I wanted, I asked myself, "What am I now doing and is it working?"

I acknowledged to myself that I was avoiding staff who seemed uninterested in the change process, staff who were critical of me, staff who were complaining about the changes. I also realized I was spending lots of time with staff who agreed with me, staff who were implementing quality school ideas, staff who showed me respect and support. Knowing how important involvement is to collaboration, I quickly answered, "No!" to the question, "If I continue to avoid staff who have a picture that is different from mine, will I be able to create the conditions for staff to resolve conflicts through collaboration?"

I thought about what I wanted to be saying to myself. "All behavior is purposeful. Everybody is doing the best they can. Change is developmental. Everyone has something important to say." There were also several things I decided to do differently. I decided to spend more time with the people I had been avoiding, to ask them about what they wanted for the school, for their classrooms, and for their students. From their wants, I would to try to identify what they needed (belonging, power, freedom, fun). I wanted to validate their pictures and needs and share with them my pictures and my needs.

I reviewed my personal strategies for conflict resolution. Raised in a conflict-averse family, I had little experience, so I arranged a half-day inservice with Diane on conflict resolution. She taught the five conflict-resolution styles outlined here. When she focused on the highest form of conflict resolution, collaboration, she stressed the importance of involvement in helping people to move from their wants to their needs and in collapsing the differing wants to create a new picture that satisfies combined needs.

She asked staff to self-evaluate. "Who are you sitting next to? Are you sitting with people who have a similar picture? Who do you usually sit next to at faculty meetings, at lunch, at staff discussions? Who do you spend time with at school? Do you share your pictures only with people who have similar pictures? Do you spend time trying to understand people with different pictures?"

This self-evaluation left a lasting impression on staff. Now at faculty meetings we remind each other about the importance of involvement in resolving conflicts. Staff interact with a wider variety of people, and people are more open about sharing their pictures, their wants, and their needs. This group made the decision to try to sit in meetings with people who were different from themselves, in order to understand them and to honor their views.

Now when I think back to this difficult time, I wish that in addition to self-evaluating privately, I could have self-evaluated publicly. Since then I have learned the power of modeling authentic self-evaluation. It not only helps to resolve conflicts, but it helps me be the kind of person I want to be—a quality leader.

SUMMARY

Whether conflict is internal or interpersonal, seek to collapse the conflict for a solution that meets all the needs in question. This is not always easy and can be accomplished consistently only in a collegial culture of involvement and respect. It requires self-evaluation and dialogue. It enriches all parties, including the organization, increasing freedom and further developing the skill and confidence needed to align practices with agreed beliefs, values, and best knowledge.

ALIGNING PRACTICES

This chapter challenges us to apply the reality test to see if what we are currently doing is aligned with what we want and what we say we believe. Our practices need also to be tested in the light of what best knowledge says. Best knowledge is both our personal experience and research. The character chosen for this chapter means sincerity, authenticity and truth. The radicals help us to understand that authenticity and truth only come when what we succeed in doing is aligned with our beliefs, that there is complete synchrony between what we say and what we do. In other words, sincerity is a sure guarantee that we will align our practices with our beliefs.

ALIGNING PRACTICES

Aligning practices is closing the gap between what you believe and what you do. Closing that gap, moving from where you are toward where you want to be, is our definition of progress. Alignment results from confronting the core reality therapy question: "Does your present behavior have a reasonable chance of getting you what you want now, and will it take you in the direction you want to go?"

Aligning practices is how schools move from theory to implementation. In the first couple of years of the change process, staff conduct dialogue about best knowledge, clarify their beliefs, create their vision of an ideal school, and establish their school's social contract. During these initial years, change is only incremental; the focus is on improving the existing structure. By about the third year of the change process, schools are ready for major changes in the way they do their work.

For many, this is where the journey towards quality ends. People begin to say things like, "Maybe we need to think about this for a while. Maybe we shouldn't do this." There is personal pain in organized abandonment—letting go of old ways that are not getting you what you want. The change process begins to slow down at this stage, when the painful details of personal change surface. "What? You mean I will have to move to another room?" might be a typical comment.

Control theory will guide you through this. Remember that your energy for change arises from the perceived gap or frustration between what you want and what you perceive you are getting. If you are not getting a perception of what you want, you act to correct the disturbance.

This corrective action may take the form of relinquishing the want or confusing the perception, but although either of these choices may reduce frustration, neither will lead to quality. To reduce frustration *and* enhance quality, plan behavior changes to align your practices with your values and beliefs.

Readers who naturally like to design back may have flipped forward to this section of the book to see what a quality school looks like after aligning its classroom practices. You might expect to see statements here regarding grading, testing, homework, discipline, curriculum, attendance, enrichment. Not finding a definite picture, you may be disappointed.

We hear this frustration from people who ask us, "What does a Quality School look like? How is a Quality School different from ours? What would we see if we visited a Quality School?" Our answers to these questions are not what people expect. They are expecting us to describe a specific program, or a set of classroom practices, or a packaged curriculum. We don't tell them about an end product, we tell them about a process.

The process involves creating the conditions for staff to self-evaluate, using the Reality Therapy Questions or the Success Connection Questions. In case these processes don't work, a problem-solving process is also reviewed in this section. Besides these processes, we describe some techniques and strategies to help staff and students figure out how to align their practices and change what they do.

The self-evaluation and planning processes, strategies, and techniques suggested in this section assume that your school has been working purposefully towards becoming a quality school for long enough to undertake all the stages of the change process outlined in the earlier sections of this book. Too many models for school change start at this stage, modifying curriculum and classroom practices; they fail because personal change and system change have not been integrated.

There are some prerequisites for effectively using the processes and strategies suggested in this section. It is important that your team have:

An understanding of the change process.

Roles and relationships that are characterized by openness, trust, and respect.

Successful experience with several group process strategies: conflict resolution, consensus-building, problem-solving.

Decided to work towards becoming a Quality School.

Read and had extensive dialogue about several books and articles on quality schools.

Received training in control theory and reality therapy.

Become knowledge-focused.

Shifted from a stimulus-response to a control theory view of the world.

Learned to self-evaluate privately and publicly.

Shifted from a congenial culture to a collegial culture.

Reached consensus on the school's purpose, beliefs, outcomes, values and ethics.

Created a shared vision of a quality school.

Learned to work together collaboratively rather than competitively.

Learned to use the Success Connection and reality therapy questions to plan how you can get more of what you want.

Does this sound like an exhaustive list? It is, and that's why aligning classroom practices begins late in the change process. Once you have met the prerequisites listed above, you are ready to go ahead in the exciting and challenging process of aligning classroom practices with beliefs, wants, and best knowledge.

The rest of this section will offer strategies, techniques, and examples that you can follow to create conditions for your team to self-evaluate, to sustain and even increase commitment to the visions developed in moving forward, while planning without fear or failure the practice and program changes that will take you in the direction you want to go.

STUDENT MANAGEMENT

One task of alignment in a Quality School is teaching control theory to the children. Schools progress towards quality when the children understand what their needs are and when teachers on a daily basis use this information to give them practice in making decisions. Trying to implement the Quality School without involving the children is like trying to manage a Little League team without introducing the players to the diamond.

When everyone has learned the language of control theory, it is easy to shift from discussing feelings and problems to analyzing needs and finding solutions. There are a variety of ways these ideas can be taught. Some of the books which will be useful are: *Control Theory in the Classroom, Teach Them To Be Happy, I'm Learning to Be Happy, In Pursuit of Happiness, My Quality World, Teachers Guide for In Pursuit of Happiness*, and *Control Theory in Action*. The Quality School believes that children learning control theory become more self-directed and self-disciplined.

TEACHING NEEDS

Begin by teaching the needs. This is fun, and children of any age can learn to identify how they are getting belonging, personal power, freedom, and fun. They can list important people or activities in each area, draw pictures to illustrate them, or create collages that represent each need.

Students also can learn their needs by exploring their quality worlds. One elementary teacher draws each child's silhouette and then invites the child to make it into a poster, filling the silhouette with quality world pictures. Children can choose songs that convey their pictures.

Once children have learned the needs, it is important to review them daily in some context. For example, they can identify needs that are revealed by characters in stories. A teacher in Truckee Elementary School made a huge cardboard hand. Each finger represented a psychological need, and the thumb represented survival. Every morning children came in and put a clothespin with their name on it on a piece of yarn attached to one of the fingers. This gave teacher Mary Yamazaki an immediate clue how to help them in the day. For example, if a lot of children had a power need identified, she would help them do work that would give immediate success.

Children can blow up balloons to represent the balance of their needs. Many small fun balloons indicates that the teacher needs to attend to the connection between learning and fun: children may see learning as work and only seek fun at recess.

Another activity for daily review of needs is having two children each day fill up clear plastic cups with rice to the level they believe their needs are met. Explaining this to the class can be an oral English or listening activity. Teachers can also model talking about how they themselves are meeting their needs.

Freedom

Aligning practices means creating a need-fulfilling environment in the classroom. One of the best ways to teach children about their need for freedom is to create the conditions for children to make lots of choices. Aligned teachers value different learning styles, and they invite children to make choices related to what they want to do and how they want to do it. This approach supports the loose/tight connection. Teachers are tight, or clear, about student outcomes, but loose, or flexible, about how students accomplish the outcomes.

A teacher at Judy's school displayed a sign in his room that read, "To be really happy you need to make choices." That teacher also lists "required work" and "choices" at the beginning of each day. The choices he offers almost always outnumber the required assignments.

When children are truly free to make choices, they are more likely to take risks. Quality teachers support risk-taking by acknowledging that people learn from mistakes. They are not afraid to make mistakes. They model restitution and purposeful behavior when they make a mistake. They say things like:

It's OK to make a mistake.

Perfection is not a human condition.

I didn't do that for no reason.

Could I have done worse? What value was I protecting? Give myself credit. What's my plan to make it better?

When teachers ask the question, "Does it really matter?" and practice "Yes, if..." management, they open up the territory for students to learn and experience freedom, just as you did for staff in getting started to reduce fear and coercion in the system.

Belonging

Belonging is fostered in the classroom by the teacher consciously offering unconditional acceptance. Too often teachers have built belonging on praise or compliments about a child's behavior. This is certainly better than criticisms, but the problem is that such a practice "twins" the belonging and power needs. As a result, children can get very nervous when they can't perform. Not only do they have a frustration in their power need, but they are unbalanced also in belonging. Where this is most obvious is with children who are academically, athletically, or musically talented. They may get very nervous about whether they can do a perfect job. That is because they are saying to themselves, "Will I be loved if I can't achieve?" Sometimes they test you by refusing to perform. They are then uncoupling their achievement to test whether they are loved.

The aligned teacher preempts this problem by validating the children as unique individuals rather than giving them approval only when they perform. An example of this is when a child says, "Look, teacher, I got a 100. Are you proud of me?" A quality teacher will ask the student to self-evaluate saying, "What do you think? Did you get what you worked for?" If pushed further, the teacher could say, "I think you did a good job, but even if you made a mistake, I'd be happy to have you in my class." A quality teacher invites students to do quality work, but also emphasizes, "Your marks are not the measure of you, the person." The teacher may say that people can have a hard time in school but do well in life.

Power

The quality school provides all students with the opportunity to achieve to meet their power needs. Students are given work they can complete, and they are given opportunities to re-do it to increase its quality. Teachers provide multisensory learning opportunities and intentionally focus on children who have abilities that are not always recognized by traditional assessment practices.

For example, one high school teacher with a gifted learning-disabled student let him demonstrate for the staff. She challenged them, "Hold his hands and ask him to spell." This boy could not spell the simplest word when his kinesthetic path was impeded. Then the teacher challenged any staff member to compete with the boy in memorizing an unrelated list of twenty words. In two minutes the boy could repeat back the total list in order, because he had perfected the pegboard system of organization. No teacher could match him.

Too often teachers identify students' learning disabilities without seeking to maximize the compensatory strategies they have developed to function in the world. Aligning practices means teaching to students' attributes rather than focusing on remediation.

When students are doing quality learning, they can see how it is useful in the real world. Alignment in a Quality School means that teachers seek to relate the curriculum to daily life and, where possible, they seek participation from community members to make this connection. For example, one Arizona high school is joint-venturing with an aircraft company to help prepare students for jobs which will open up at the turn of the century.

Fun

Fun is the genetic reward for learning. Alignment with control theory means helping students find fun in class rather than just at recess. Traditionally there has been an artificial separation between work and fun. Alignment means erasing this line.

Two Australian teachers, Judi Byrnes and Kay Collier, report that a substitute teacher told them she felt guilty about getting paid because the only problem she had was the children wanting to stay in at recess and work on their projects. Judy and Kay say homework is no problem, because children are anxious to show their parents what they are learning and to ask for their help to find more resources. Going into their joint classroom of sixty students is a treat because it is difficult to find these teachers. They are crouched on the floor with the children, who are engrossed in their projects.

In Quality Schools, teachers can also get more fun for themselves by using the self-evaluation questions "Does it really matter?" and "Could it be worse?" This helps keep things in perspective and invites consideration of the roads not yet traveled.

Teaching Behavior

Once they know about needs, students can learn how to manage their behavioral cars. Dr. Glasser's analogy of a behavioral car helps students understand their total behavior. On the control theory chart the four wheels of the car represent the four components of behavior: action, thinking, feeling, and physiology. Teachers explain that if students want to gain effective control of their behavior, rather than "spin on their back wheels" (feeling and physiology) they can "steer their behavior car" with two from wheels (acting and thinking). Dr. Glasser teaches us to never talk to children about their feelings without connecting it to the front wheels where they have control. Examples are asking, *When you feel mad, what are you thinking?* or *What are you doing when you feel depressed?*

A primary student once spent fifteen minutes teaching Dr. Glasser how he managed his behavior on the playground, using a behavior car made with film spools and popsicle sticks he had hung around his neck. He had experienced many suspensions from his classroom the previous year, but he reported that this year was better after his teacher taught their class the car of life.

As he fingered the front spool he said, "When I feel my body talk on my back wheels getting loud, I have to hold on to my front wheels and think about my need and what I can say to myself and do." This boy has learned self-discipline, and his teacher seldom uses consequences to monitor his behavior. He also has taught the car to his mother, who helps him with it at home.

Larry Larson, a high school counselor for the Saskatoon Public School Board, ran an aftercare program for students who had been in treatment for addictions. This program was established because very few of these students were being successful. They spent one class period per day learning control theory.

In Larry's class they learned about their behavior car and how it related to their addiction. They learned how to identify when they were getting tense on their physiology wheel, to analyze the need not met, and to plan with the support of the group to meet their need responsibly.

They also did weekly tune-ups on their cars. They drew customized versions of their cars, adding any accessories needed to make them run smoothly, such as defoggers to help with denial. This program was aligned because it was teaching the students control theory and because the teacher was involving the students in solving their own problems.

DISCIPLINE

A key element for creating a Quality School is the shift from discipline based on suffering consequences for breaking rules the students have nothing to do with creating to discipline based on self-evaluating, learning better things to, and classroom agreements that they themselves have had a say in creating. In life we have to follow laws, but the laws are made by elected legislators who have to make an effort to create acceptable laws or risk defeat.

Good citizens do not obey laws solely because of the consequences; they obey them mostly because, based on self-evaluation, this is the sensible thing to do. The more a school follows the practices of the real world, the more children will learn to deal effectively with that world.

If children break their own rules, the only consequences should be removal from the situation and counseling. Punitive consequences are not effective because they do not teach better behaviors. Control Theory teaches that we cannot stop behaviors which break rules, we can only learn new and better behaviors based on beliefs we all agree on.

For example, in *Schools Without Failure* (New York: Harper Collins, 1975), Dr. Glasser advocated involving students in setting up their own rules and consequences. He said that a school had to offer the students something to invest in: a school which was not need-satisfying would not be a place where students would choose to behave. He suggested that all students should know the rules and that the rules be stated in the positive and be enforceable. Students need to know the consequences, and when a rule has been broken, something must happen. A Quality School recognizes this and adds self-evaluation and the reality therapy technique of restitution as the missing piece of the discipline puzzle.

Restitution

In a quality school teachers learn the reality therapy technique of restitution, which is used when it is possible for the students, in line with their personal values, to restore something any student may have taken away from the group. For example, a second grade boy flushed another student's key ring down the toilet. The boy's plan to fix the problem was to take money out of his savings account and replace the key ring. Teachers learn to be managers rather than monitors. Teachers who continue to act as monitors ask: "What's the rule? What's the consequence? What did you do? What happens to you now?" The questions for the manager are: "What do we believe? Do you believe it? If you believe it, do you want to fix the situation? If you decide to fix it, will that help you become the kind of person you want to be?"

As you can tell by the questions asked, the role of the manager is quite different from the role of the monitor. The monitor seeks conformity from the students. The manager wants to assist students to create a reparation which will leave them not just exonerated but feeling stronger. The manager is not happy to see students discomforted or to hear them say, "I'll do it for *you*." The shift from monitoring to managing is the shift from external discipline to internal discipline. It accompanies the shift from stimulus-response thinking to control-theory thinking.

Quality School teachers learn about the five positions of control—punisher, guilter, buddy, monitor, and manager. They think about how they were disciplined as children and evaluate what they learned from these adult interventions in their lives. They then assess their current practices with students. Frequently they find that they are teaching students how to conform, to apologize, and to do detention after school.

One principal said, "If the students are doing all these things and we are getting what we want, why would we want to change it?" This question sparked a vigorous discussion in the group, for it led to reaffirming a basic principle of the quality school that says our exit outcome is self-directing and self-disciplining students. A self-disciplined student is doing more than complying. A self-disciplined student behaves even when there is no monitor. Self-disciplined students self-restitute. They understand that their first duty is to themselves, the second is to the party wronged.

Using the Reality Therapy Questions to Align Discipline Practices

Significant changes in school practices evolve through a process of staff intentionally self-evaluating, using the reality therapy questions.

What do we want?

What are we doing?

Is it working?

What is our plan to get more of what we want?

These questions sound simple, but when you create the conditions for a group to come together to ask themselves these questions, the result is a powerful process for aligning what you do with what you want, know, and believe.

The following example shows how the Sheridan Hills staff used the reality therapy questions to align their discipline practices with their wants, their beliefs, and their knowledge about human behavior. Because the process is so powerful and because it incorporates nearly all the skills and concepts we have offered here, we present this example in some depth to demonstrate the role of the reality therapy questions in creating conditions for aligning practices.

What Do We Want?

In 1992, Sheridan Hills appeared to have solved the discipline puzzle with a good program of positive discipline. Parents and visitors to the school would have asked, "Why change anything?" The children appeared well-behaved. The discipline plan was clearly communicated to students and parents. Administration, staff, students, and parents felt the school was safe and orderly. Staff had extensive training in the philosophy and methods of the program. Staff had ownership in the design of the discipline plan. There was a crisis-intervention plan for unusual situations involving a student in crisis.

But staff had become uncomfortable. Following the program described in Getting Started, they recently had gained new knowledge about control theory, reality therapy, and the technique of restitution. As a result of this new knowledge, their wants had changed, along with their beliefs and values about human behavior. Their new pictures were reflected in questions like these:

What do we believe about intrinsic and extrinsic rewards?

Do we have to punish students to teach them a lesson?

What will students do if we don't give them rewards for being good?

What will students do if we stop using praise to control them?

Can we make students do something they really don't want to do?

How can a misbehavior be a purposeful behavior?

How can we help students move from a failure identity to a success identity?

The energy level of staff was high during their discussion of the question, "What do we want?" Staff were invited to brainstorm in small groups about their pictures of how staff and students would treat each other. They talked about what they would see and hear and how people would feel. They explored what it would mean to them if that happened. They shared their personal beliefs and values. They asked themselves, "Is our picture consistent with the district's belief statements and the exit outcomes for all learners?"

The ideal picture of how the staff wanted to see people treating themselves and each other at Sheridan Hills included the following ideas:

Showing respect for ourselves, others, our work, and our environment.

Caring about each other and being loved unconditionally; feeling like a family.

Understanding that we are internally motivated.

Satisfying our needs.

Shifting from positive reinforcement to self-evaluation.

Believing it's OK to make a mistake.

Shifting from consequences to restitution.

Exercising and valuing freedom, without fear and coercion.

Fixing our own problems.

Being self-disciplined.

Shifting from violent to peaceful.

Resolving conflicts through collaboration.

After the planning day, staff commented enthusiastically about the process: "This was the best faculty meeting I have ever attended. It was exciting to create a vision of how we wanted our school to be. Discussing our beliefs helped us reach common ground from which we could take action."

What Are We Doing?

Clear on what they wanted, staff looked at what they were doing, where they were and where they had been. Five years ago the school had had an assertive discipline plan in place. This plan was based on stimulus-response theory. It included rules, consequences, and rewards.

At first this plan had worked well, but each year staff had become more dissatisfied. The following comments were common: "We have to offer bigger and better rewards each year. Students want to know what they will get before they decide whether something is worth doing. Check marks on the board don't work for the students who are disruptive, and the other students don't need them. What's the plan for students who don't care about check marks? Why do students need a reward for doing what is expected of them? What do we do in a crisis?"

In response to these frustrations, staff had decided in 1990 to revise their discipline plan. They had received additional training in passive restraint, and the school organized a crisis-intervention team. The school had replaced the assertive discipline plan with the positive discipline plan. All staff had received training in this highly stimulus-response program.

The positive discipline philosophy emphasized the importance of making it pay to behave. Each student had a tally chart for recording smiley faces earned for following the three school rules: work, respect, and belong. Teachers stamped smiley faces on students' charts when they followed these rules. Students could receive smiley-face coupons in the lunchroom, on the playground, and going out to the bus at dismissal. There were weekly awards, certificates, and incentives for earning these faces. Then at the end of the month students could use these smiley faces to buy things at an auction. Besides the smiley faces, there were blank faces and sad faces for students who were not following the rules. A letter home to parents stated, "Self-discipline is fostered when we make it pay to behave."

Looking at where they were and how they had gotten there, staff said yes to "Could we be doing worse?" Positive discipline did represent progress, and they affirmed that they had done a good job of learning and applying it. They had selected the program thoughtfully and they were operating it well. There still remained the question, "Is it working?"

Is It Working?

The positive discipline plan had worked well at first, just like the assertive discipline plan, but the novelty wore off more quickly. Students figured out the system very quickly, and these students were only in grades kindergarten through third! Students were reproducing fake smiley faces, trading faces, stealing them, and even using them for extortion. A student would agree to stop teasing another student in exchange for one of the smiley faces. This is consistent with Alfie's Kohn's comments in his book, *Punished by Rewards* (p. 54):

> At best rewards do nothing to promote collaboration or a sense of community. More often, they actually interfere with these goals: an undercurrent of "strifes and jealousies" is created whenever people scramble for goodies.

Students with severe behavior problems were getting more smiley faces and receiving the special rewards because teachers had to pay them more to be good.

Many teachers had stopped giving the smiley faces and modified the program unilaterally to meet their own needs. Some teachers commented: "Many students don't care if they get smiley faces. The students who do care become angry and jealous of others who get faces. I'm spending too much time counting smiley faces. This plan works when I'm in the room, but if I leave the room or have a substitute teacher the plan doesn't work."

In these and similar observations we heard the answers to some specific is-it-working questions:

Are we promoting self-discipline?

Are we reducing fear and coercion?

Are we providing opportunities for students to fix their own problems?

Are we fostering self-evaluation?

Are we teaching conflict-resolution?

The major concern of staff, though, was that the positive discipline plan was not aligned with their beliefs, their exit outcomes for all learners, and their new knowledge about control theory and restitution. Most importantly it was not aligned with their ideal picture of how they wanted their school to be. Teachers were using positive reinforcement and praise to control students. Teachers were monitors of consequences instead of managers of restitutions. Teachers used fear and coercion to try to control students. Students were not encouraged to fix their own problems.

To the question, "Is what we're doing aligned with our knowledge and values?" they answered no. It was not aligned with our desire to help students become more self-directed. They were teaching students to conform rather than creating the conditions for them to learn self-discipline. They were also creating the conditions for students to choose to behave for reward or to avoid punishment rather than for self-respect. Their current discipline plan did not match the belief that children are internally motivated. Because staff thus perceived a need for change, they were ready and willing to make a plan for change together.

What is Our Plan to Get More of What We Want?

The Sheridan Hills staff, focusing on their ideal picture of what they wanted and recognizing that what they were doing wasn't working, asked, "What can we agree to do together to get what we want?" They began to try some of the ideas they had learned in the two-day workshop on control theory, reality therapy, and the Quality School.

Staff were eager to shift from monitoring rules and consequences to managing restitutions. As teachers began to lead students to make restitutions, there were many creative solutions. Teachers enthusiastically exchanged with one another their students' restitution plans. Students became interested in fixing their own mistakes.

But as the novelty wore off, several concerns surfaced. Staff found students slow to respond to the question, "What do we believe?" Since this question is the starting point in helping a child make a restitution, no answer—from a student looking confused—made it difficult to proceed. Teachers began to complain about the amount of time required to plan a restitution and the burden of managing too many restitutions.

As staff examined their concerns, they discussed the importance of establishing the social contract or classroom agreement. In retrospect, staff realized it is better to help students create restitutions tied to beliefs. They had opened up the territory, set the limits, established the roles, and moved to restitution before creating a common picture of the ideal classroom based on beliefs and values.

In planning for a new school year, staff agreed to focus more on establishing the social contract. They decided to embrace a shared, school-wide, belief: **At Sheridan Hills we respect ourselves, others, our work, and our environment. Together we are the best we can be.**

This belief would not just be for the students. Staff would model this belief in their interactions with other staff, with parents, and with students. They would ask these questions of themselves and of students who violated the social contract:

What do we believe?

What is our picture of the ideal classroom?

What are the common values we agreed on as a class?

What kind of a person do you want to be?

What is your plan to make it right?

Personalizing the school-wide belief statement, each classroom would establish a classroom agreement. Through dialogue about their values and beliefs, students would build a common picture of how they wanted to work together in the classroom. From their dialogue, students would establish a classroom agreement. Each agreement would be unique, but the theme of respect and working as a team would be a common focus.

This planning process helped staff reach a common picture of how they wanted people to treat each other. They also reached consensus on the basic structure of the discipline plan, but they had different pictures of how they would build it in their classrooms. It was important for staff to have the freedom to select materials and plan lessons to teach the ideas of control theory and reality therapy, and they needed to individualize the classroom dialogues. While holding tightly to agreed values, beliefs, and outcomes, they planned only loosely how their discipline plan would be developed in the classrooms. Samples of the resulting classroom agreements are in Appendix *B*.

With these classroom agreements as the focal point, Sheridan Hills continued to help students self-evaluate and solve their own problems without anyone getting hurt.

SUMMARY

Teaching control theory to students and aligning discipline practices helps to create a warm and supportive environment. Self-evaluation and using the technique of restitution establishes a non-coercive environment where students solve problems out of respect for self rather than to avoid pain or to gain approval.

Managing students without coercion, however, is not enough to ensure that students are doing quality work. You also will examine, "What is it that we ask students to do?" The answer to this question moves you into the next phase of becoming a Quality School, the "integration phase," where you focus on how the curriculum changes so that students do quality work because what you ask them to do adds quality to their lives.

Curriculum

Creating a quality environment by teaching students control theory and managing them without fear and coercion is but one aspect of alignment. Creating a quality curriculum is also an exciting challenge. The process is the same—to affirm and sustain your vision of quality while evaluating practices and adopting changes consistent with your beliefs and values, ethics, knowledge, and desired outcomes.

Like the reality therapy process delineated above, we have found the Success Connection to be useful for alignment. There also are some specific strategies and activities which create conditions for self-evaluation leading to change.

Success Connection Questions

The Success Connection—described in Moving Forward to identify wants, beliefs, and knowledge—can also be adapted to guide alignment of classroom practices. These questions, when used intentionally, can create the conditions for self-evaluation leading to significant change.

In the following example, the Success Connection questions are addressed to evaluating a reading program.

Figure 17. Success Connection Questions

Question 1   Is what we are doing now getting us what we want?

Question 2   What do we really want in regard to teaching reading? (What is our vision?)

Question 3   In regard to teaching reading, what are our present practices, actions, behaviors?

Question 4   What experiences, knowledge, research will help us figure out how to achieve our wants?

Question 5   How does our new knowledge influence our present beliefs in regard to teaching reading?

Question 6   Which present practices need to be changed so that they align with our wants, what we know, and what we believe?

Developed by Arthur J. Chambers, Johnson City Central Schools,
December, 1991

Judy's Story of Using the Success Connection Questions to Align the Reading Program

At this stage of our change process, we used the loose/tight connectors (purpose, beliefs, values, outcomes, ethics, and knowledge) to screen all our ideas, checking for alignment. We made all our decisions based on these connectors. To stimulate and sustain positive change, we used the Success Connection questions.

These questions served as a framework for dialogue to reach consensus for a plan of action at several levels. At the district level, these questions formed the basis for the North Central Accreditations self-study process. A district-wide committee answered these questions in formulating a plan to improve technology with funding from a successful bond referendum. At the building level, staff used these questions to clarify their reading program.

Initially we were skeptical, because this was a controversial topic. There was a polarization among the staff regarding the use of a basal reading approach or a whole language approach. In retrospect, my advice would be to select a less controversial practice or program for your first attempt with this process. Despite the controversy, however, we found that the Success Connection allowed us to maintain and perhaps increase our involvement with one another as we struggled toward resolution.

The Process

In preparation for the discussion of our reading program, we ordered from the North Central Association's Gold File the best knowledge and research on how children learn to read. This literature and research were available for all staff to read and discuss.

The Success Connection questions were important, but the process used to answer the questions was most powerful. We used the Success Connection questions as a guide for our dialogue.

We created the conditions for maximum individual involvement and ownership. Initial discussion groups consisted of two to four people, to encourage individual input. When each small group reached consensus, they would join another group to reach a larger consensus.

Each discussion group would identify a recorder/reporter and a process observer. The task of the recorder/reporter was to record and report the information that the group reached consensus on. The process observer would redirect the group if they were off-task or were using killer phrases ("We've never done it that way." "We've tried that before." "It's against our school policy.").

When groups with four to eight people reached consensus, they would record their ideas for visual presentation to the entire staff (flipchart paper, transparencies, copies, etc.). Once the five or six groups shared their ideas, we considered a variety of group-process strategies for reaching consensus.

A smaller committee drafts a combined list, eliminating duplications.

Each smaller group prioritizes its ideas and then gives one idea at a time, in turn, until all ideas are offered to the larger group. As each smaller group contributes, others eliminate similar ideas from their lists, preventing duplications.

Small-group representatives form a consensus circle. There is a chair for the designated spokesperson of each smaller group, plus two extra chairs. Other staff sit around this inner circle of chairs. As the circle works to reach consensus, anyone from the larger group may sit in one of the two empty chairs to contribute. Substitutions in the consensus circle may be scheduled or spontaneous.

The Outcome

Reflecting on best knowledge from the literature and our experience helped us clarify our beliefs. In clarifying our beliefs and establishing our common ground, our differences became insignificant and irrelevant. When teachers explained how they taught reading, others were more receptive, developing new pictures for themselves by combining seemingly incompatible pictures.

Staff began to influence each other at a higher level. Diversity among ideas and practices came to be valued rather than feared. Respect and trust were strengthened. Staff began to self-evaluate rather than evaluate others.

Staff began to understand the importance of the loose/tight connectors. They were tight on their beliefs, values, and outcomes for children learning to read, but they stayed loose on the implementation of the reading program.

Clarifying values and beliefs sets the stage for change. Living the beliefs influences classroom practices. If you know what you want, then you can intentionally choose what you do based on best knowledge.

REFLECTING IN ACTION

Challenge your staff to adopt what Donald Schon calls "reflecting in action." This means that one pays attention to what one is doing while doing it and thinking about how it is working. This could also be called "control theory in action."

When we speak of alignment, we need to begin with ourselves. We need to create ways for staff to use control theory in a meaningful, ongoing, process-oriented manner. There are three resources which can assist you. One is the Workplace Needs Survey with computer software by Jeffrey A. Mintz (Institute for Management Development, Inc., 1992) which assists staff in assessing their training needs. For ongoing daily journaling and self -evaluation by teachers, *The Journey to Quality* (Chapel Hill: New View, 1992) by Mona Perdue and Mariwyn Tinsley offers many practical ideas. Shelley Brierley and colleagues out of Oasis Consulting in Vancouver, British Columbia, have developed a four-day process-oriented workshop which really helps staff learn to work in teams. Each of these resources can help you as a leader create the conditions for staff to move to become a learning organization. Never ask staff to do with students anything they do not personally find is helpful. Before they teach their classes they need to be learners of new ways. Create opportunities for dialogue about what they are learning.

In support of the reality therapy or Success Connection process, or at any time to address a specific problem, question, or conflict of alignment, there are some specific group process techniques that help create conditions for self-evaluation and maintain involvement while increasing alignment.

One way you can create the conditions for staff to reflect while teaching is to provide teachers with best knowledge and time for dialogue about their beliefs and practices. Reflecting on best knowledge from the literature and experience helps clarify pictures, examine practices, and evaluate effectiveness. It also serves to guide planning for change when staff find that what they are doing is not working to take them where they want to go. Help your staff gain constant access to current best knowledge. As they internalize best knowledge, they begin to question their beliefs and classroom practices.

To initiate dialogue for reflection about classroom practices, offer a handout like the one at Figure 18. It is a continuum chart for change appropriate for primary-grade programs. It reflects the most current knowledge of teaching and learning as derived from theory, research, and practice.

Figure 18. **New Paradigm for Primary Schools (K-3) Continuum of Change for Curriculum**

From	To
Graded	Ungraded
Separate subjects	Integrated subjects
Workbooks	Concrete materials, quality literature, and a variety of resource materials
Prescribed sequence (lock-step)	Developmental sequence (variable)
Established (preset) material	School/teacher determined
Focus on "3 R's"	Focus on attitudes, concepts, skills, and processes
Limited multicultural content	Expanded multicultural content
Work and play divided	Play is a type of work for young learners
Fixed daily schedule	Flexible time
Limited outdoor activity	Outdoor activity planned daily
Health taught via textbooks and posters	Variety of health and safety projects
Limited time to practice social skills	Many daily opportunities to practice social skills
Art, music and physical education taught as special subjects once a week	Art, music, physical education, and other physical activities are integrated daily
Reading taught as discrete subject using basal readers; language, writing, and spelling workbooks	Whole language to develop and expand ability to communicate verbally and through meaningful reading & writing
Math as separate subject using textbooks, workbooks, worksheets, and board work	Math through exploration, discovery, and solving meaningful problems

Sporadic social studies instruction usually related to holidays, commercially developed weekly paper, or activities from social studies textbook	Social studies themes are focus of work for extended periods of time
Science taught from single textbook with use of workbooks; learning is primarily via memorization	Discovery science is emphasized with science projects experimental, exploratory, and actively involving every child

Floyd McDowell, *"Developmentally Appropriate Primary Phase Education and School Improvement,"* Quality Outcomes-Driven Education

There are several other strategies and techniques that you can use to challenge staff to reflect on their beliefs and practices. Teachers can identify areas to improve upon and then work on them one at a time. Or a faculty can identify two or three areas and develop a school-wide improvement plan.

You can help one another reflect in action by calling attention to observations that appear out of alignment with desired outcomes, agreed beliefs, or best knowledge. Challenge your staff by asking alignment questions and inviting them to self-evaluate: "If this is what I see, what belief does this reflect?" Here are a few examples that show common practices and the undesired belief they reflect.

Practice: Teacher lecturing in front of class the majority of time

Belief: Knowledge input is the role of the teacher

Practice: Students doing worksheets, busy work

Belief: Students learn alone, repetition is important

Practice: Teacher putting trick questions on a test

Belief: Purpose of testing is to sort kids, determine letter grades

Conversely, you may ask: "Here's the belief. What will I see or not see?" Invite staff to identify their beliefs and then ask themselves, "What would I be doing?" and "What would I not be doing." Through this self-evalua-tion process, teachers can recognize where their class-room practices are not aligned with their beliefs. Here is an ex-ample of a desired belief with an aligned classroom practice ("See") and an unaligned classroom practice ("Not See").

Belief: Process is important, not facts.

See: Teachers put answers on the board, check process, have answer keys available for students.

Not See: Check answers next day.

T-Charts

The T-Chart activity is yet another technique to help staff focus on the alignment of their classroom practices with their beliefs. The T-chart we use to focus on align-ment has two columns, "See" and "Not See." Staff select a belief on which they have reached consensus. In pairs they dialogue about what they would "see" and "not see" if that belief were practiced. Then pairs share their ideas with the entire faculty and together they make a large T-Chart like the one below.

For example, this is what a T-Chart might include for the belief that **Pupils' rates of learning may vary from task to task. We are committed to keep opportunities open and support available.**

Figure 19. **Beliefs in Practice**	
See	**Not See**
Variable time opportunities	Inflexible grouping
Support for extended learning	Sameness in teaching
Reteach using a different method	Uniformity in amount of material or time

Take Control Chart

Once staff understand the Take Control Chart, they can use it to focus and facilitate alignment of practices, individually and as a group. Judy recalls how Sheridan Hills followed the Take Control planning process to evaluate and align their writing process.

We were **feeling** incompetent and frustrated about the fact that our students weren't writing freely. We **felt** lack of energy. What we heard that we **didn't want** was, "What will I write? How many words does it have to be? What do you want me to write about?" What we **wanted** to be hearing from students was, "When are we going to write about our weekend?" or "I'm glad I brought along my journal so I can remember this trip," or "I want to write about my basketball game!" or "Let's write about how we solved our math problem."

We analyzed our wants and recognized an underlying **need** to be competent, to gain personal power. Trying to persuade the students was not working, so we needed a new **plan**. Our **plan** was to review best knowledge and obtain some expert advice. Our **strategy** for doing this was to invite a consultant to advise us.

Figure 20. **Take Control Chart**

Problem	1. Bad Feeling	2. Don't Want
Control Theory Understanding	3. Do Want	4. Need
Solution	5. Plan	6. Strategy

Six months later, when the consultant returned to review our progress, we had started a publishing center to organize contributions from our young authors. Our frustration had diminished and we no longer felt incompetent. Our students were enthusiastically learning to write, and we were excited by their success.

SUMMARY

Alignment is an ongoing process of continuing to self-evaluate: "Does our present behavior have a reasonable chance of getting us what we want now and will it take us in the direction we want to go?" Alignment is a never-ending journey of self-renewal, calling upon all the skills, knowledge, and environmental strength achieved earlier in the developmental process of change.

CONTINUING RENEWAL

The proverb chosen to describe the essence of this chapter is made up of two radicals. The first radical has the connotation of cycles. It is used to describe the hours of the day and night, or the seasons of the year. The second radical means "newness." It describes fresh starts and new beginnings. Together, the proverb they form gives a picture of a "cyclical rebirth" that gives rise to cycles of new beginnings. Quality leaders, in their leadership journey, continue to be reborn as they develop greater complexity of understanding. Even though circumstances might be similar, there is a newness to their approach because of this continuous evolution. This cycle of rebirth is as certain as the arrival of spring after winter, or the arrival of a new dawn after the darkest night. The security of this certainty enables the quality leader to be proactive and courageous because it is certain that new strength, insights and skills will be developed and will be accessible when the needs arise.

Continuing Renewal

Renewal is intentionally continuing to close the gap between what you know and what you are doing. It is not settling at any point of alignment. It means never being satisfied to stop where you are, always thinking there is one more place to go.

Carl Glickman confirms this in his book *Renewing America's Schools.* In summarizing the qualities of successful schools, one of the startling results he shares is that the most successful schools had the highest rates of teacher dissatisfaction with their teaching. This seems just the opposite of what conventional wisdom would predict.

Why would successful schools have high levels of dissatisfaction? It appears to result from the continuous search for quality. Teachers in successful schools never feel they have arrived. They always are aware of the potential for improvement. They continually self-evaluate and find they're not yet where they want to be. This mismatch between where they want to be and where they currently are gives both the dissatisfaction reading and impetus for changing it.

Glickman says complacency occurs in schools where teachers fail to look at themselves. He says that schools which emphasize how good they are are mainly concerned with how good they **look**. Schools concerned with how good they can **become** practice continuing renewal.

This is consistent with our experience and our knowledge of control theory. If it is the mismatch between perception and picture which generates energy for improvement, then surely complacency is antithetical to quality. In a quality school, the environment is calm but never smug. This only can be achieved with care; it takes time, effort, patience, and commitment.

Our experience has been that many schools spend a couple of years working very seriously on the first two stages of change. They gain lots of new knowledge about Quality School ideas, learn group-process skills, and create a shared vision of what they agree to become together. These stages of the change process are exciting and people enjoy them.

By the third year, however, when alignment questions begin to arise, people may withdraw from what can seem a personal threat. Ignorance is no longer bliss. They may get discouraged by examining classroom practices and answering, "Is what we're doing aligned with what we know, what we want, and what we believe?"

At this difficult and sometimes painful stage, people may begin to say, "Let's think about this a while longer. We need more information. Maybe this isn't what we want."

As we have seen, your organization can survive this stage by reliance upon earlier developmental strengths and coming to grips with alignment as a process not an event.

If your organization does move successfully past the dangers of being deterred by these negatives, however, it still will face the danger of being deterred by the positives: internal relief of discomfort and external admiration of success. As alignment occurs in a quality environment, a school begins to be noticed. When visitors come to see what's happening, there is a danger of becoming who they say you are, of wanting to look good, rather than refocusing and continuing to grow. At this stage, rather than succumbing to sheer relief or to others' accolades, ask again, "What do we want to become?"

It will be your job intentionally to ask and carefully to support this question through maintaining and strengthening courage, remaining proactive, increasing comfort with cognitive complexity, and gaining deeper understanding of the concept of self-restitution.

Continuing renewal, escaping the tendency to "get back to normal" and avoiding complacency in the face of approval, will both call upon and enhance all the control theory knowledge, all the involvement and problem-solving skills, and all the collegial habits developed during the earlier years. With such care, the renewal process can be a continuous celebration.

THE SPIRAL OF LEARNING

Just as we introduced this study by orienting you to the promises and pitfalls of change, we conclude it by introducing a higher level of understanding the change process: homeorhesis.

STAGES OF LEARNING

The stages of learning (which is, after all, what change is about) are typically represented as a linear sequence.

Figure 21. **Stages of Learning**

Unconscious Incompetence	Conscious Incompetence	Conscious Competence	Unconscious Competence
I	II	III	IV

According to this model, people go through different stages of learning. When you are doing something "wrong" but don't know a better way, you are in Stage I, at the unconscious incompetence phase of learning. For example, if no one told you it was incorrect to use a salad fork to eat your main course, you would proceed blissfully unaware of your faux pas.

Once you have information about a better way to do something, you move into Stage II, conscious incompetence, where you experience considerable frustration when comparing what you are doing with what you now recognize would be more desirable. This is the most painful stage. You see that there is a better way but haven't mastered it.

With practice, you begin to personalize the new information and to master competence, and you move into Stage III, conscious competence. Through deliberate effort, you can now both remember to use your dinner fork and use it with some safety, if not real grace. At this stage of learning, you are at the cookbook level. It is not possible to vary the process or make an application to new situations. Depending upon the complexity of the new learning, this phase can be brief or prolonged as you experience the consequences of changing practices and learn to adjust.

The final phase of learning in this model is Stage IV, unconscious competence. The new skill has been mastered and internalized, and it can now be generalized with some appropriateness. You need not pay close attention to the sequences but merely can give your behavior system an instruction to use the new competency. Practices in this phase of learning are habituated or automatic, allowing ease and efficiency of program operation.

We think this model is not quite complete. Reflect upon your own experience with even a simple skill. Over time, it tends to decay, does it not? Have you ever tried to teach someone to do something you know well, only to discover you've been leaving out a step? Have you ever improved a skill by noticing how someone even more expert does it differently?

We believe the concept of homeorhesis more accurately describes learning around a constantly reorganizing perception of excellence. Whenever a practice is mastered at a higher level of competence, the reference perception also is affected, one becomes aware of yet a better way, and the cycle begins anew. Renewal is continuous.

HOMEORHESIS

Continuing renewal views learning as an evolution, not as a continuum but as a spiral, comparable to the process described by J. G. Miller. This process is different from homeostasis, which is stability around a fixed point. Homeorhesis is stability around a point which is itself moving.

An example of homeostasis is the human body. There are set reference levels for all the physical functions in order for the body to be in balance. For example, the body changes its behavior, opening and contracting the pores to maintain the body temperature of 98.6 degrees Fahrenheit or 37 degrees Celsius. Blood can be diverted from digestion if necessary to do this. Homeostasis is like a thermostat which controls for input, varying its "behavior" to maintain a static temperature.

Homeorhesis, on the other hand, is the maintenance of equilibrium about a trajectory in time and space. Just as satisfaction of biological needs depends upon homeostasis, psychological needs are maintained by homeorhesis.

Your values are constantly changing. They are not as they were last year because you are always adding new pictures to your album and adjusting your perceptions accordingly. Continuous learning is the way you maintain equilibrium around a changing view of the world, which is itself changing. That is why we believe that in Quality Schools organizational change is continuous.

The way the brain is organized, as soon as you make a concept your own, it begins to show you another level of perception or another direction to explore. For example, a teacher approached Diane about a book he was writing on group dynamics. He asked for her opinion because he felt both that the scope of his topic was overwhelming him and that he hadn't begun to plumb the depths of his experience.

Her advice to him was to put to paper immediately that which he understood at that time—his current perception. She urged him to do this because, she assured him, what was so germane for him at that moment would have become a year later so habituated a perception that he would no longer be able to perceive its uniqueness nor convey the excitement of his insight. Although a year hence he would have a more sophisticated perception, he would be beyond the audience waiting to receive that which he had to offer.

When you are truly in touch with your potential to grow through intellectual reorganization, you will understand that, at least for the moment, change is the nymph which ever beckons, and she is a chameleon. This is homeorhesis. It explains what Robert Pirsig calls dynamic quality. Quality is a moving target.

What does homeorhesis have to do with the process of becoming a quality organization? The visual metaphor for homeorhesis is a spiral. It represents the journey towards quality. As schools move through the stages of change—getting started, moving forward, getting unstuck, aligning practices, and finally, continuing renewal—their understanding of quality reaches a new level of perception, and the cycle of change continues. The figure below illustrates this.

Figure 22. **Homeorhesis Spiral**

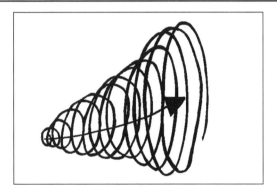

As you become aware of each new perception, you seek new information which leads to personal change. This enables new applications in the system, which then supports management changes toward better task alignment. This impact of this new alignment has consequences which call forth stronger collaboration. Ultimately you arrive at still another new level of perception, you become aware of that, and begin the cycle yet again. This is a rising spiral of aspiration, competence, and continuing renewal.

SELF-EVALUATION

Remember that every behavior is meeting a need. Rather than say to yourself, "I should have done better," ask, "Could I have done worse?" Keep yourself in the success identity, using your energy to solve problems rather than assign blame. Validate what was important to you even though you don't like how you attained it.

Recognize the purposefulness of your behavior. After recognizing what you could have done worse, identify the value you were protecting. Ask yourself what you wanted at the time. Identify how it was important to you. Identify the need you were trying to fulfill. This is not the same as saying your misbehavior was good. It is understanding yourself in order to do better.

You can also self-evaluate by backing up.

Do I believe people can learn to behave in better ways?

Do I believe this person can learn a better way?

If what this person is doing is the best that has been figured out so far, how can I help figure out a new way to meet that need which is not disruptive of my need?

Do I want to do this?

If I am able to do this, how will it be better for me?

If I don't choose to do this, what will happen?

Is this what I want?

What behaviors could I choose to use that would further aggravate the situation?

Why might I use these behaviors?

What need might they meet for me?

Should I not meet my need?

Do I want to learn a better way?

Do I believe I am a person who can learn a better way?

Understanding yourself through self-evaluation can increase your compassion for those you work with in the change process. Behaviors that are annoying can become instructive. As you use these ideas on yourself, you will make better decisions. You will find that instead of disciplining yourself to do things you don't want to do, you create new conditions in which to operate so that you have less conflict. Never accept "No" as the only answer to, "Is this helping?" Search out the "Yes" answer and try to meet your recognized needs in more responsible ways.

For example, procrastination may appear dysfunctional, but only until it becomes clear it is a way to avoid facing a task that is too difficult. Lowering expectations reduces the fear of failure, and movement forward becomes easier. This is a change from self-discipline. Clear the obstacle rather than whipping the horse.

As you recognize the purposefulness of your own behaviors, you will learn to see it in others as well. Instead of quietly raging or sulking at colleagues' behavior, become quiet detectives seeking to find the less desirable options avoided by the difficult behaviors. Grow more patient and more skilled by seeking the values being protected and using that step backward to go forward into self-evaluation.

Self-evaluation helps you continue your personal renewal. Al Mamary stresses the importance of creating a self-managing system. He suggests six questions you can ask to determine whether you are practicing true self-management.

Figure 23. **Self-evaluation for Renewal**

---

1. Am I always self-inspecting in order to produce quality? Is this my personal best at this time?

2. Am I always striving to get better?

3. Is my mind always open to new ideas and knowledge?

4. Am I modeling quality and encouraging those around me to produce quality?

5. Am I seeking feedback from others as support for getting better?

6. Am I continuously assessing my performance against agreed-upon publicly stated standards?

Al Mamary, *A Framework for Quality Learning.*

Keep asking yourself, "What kind of a person do I want to be?" This question is a source of continuous self-renewal. Rather than behave to avoid pain or to gain approval or reward from others, learn to behave for respect of self. You need not be afraid to take risks once you know that you can make a restitution when you make a mistake.

A Terrible, Horrible, Awful, No Good, Very Bad Day

Diane tells of a day when she was working with the playground supervisors at Sheridan Hills. Her job was to help them explore what they liked and what suggestions they had for change. They had several recommendations for improving the lunchroom supervision.

1. Redesign the system to reduce noise and foster self-discipline.

   Put a green signal to let kids know it's OK to go outside.

   Reverse the scheduled sequence of recess and eating.

   Feed half the grade at one time.

2. Use consequences for misbehavior when warnings have been ignored.

   Plates up to front.

   Heads down.

3. Amplify the lunchroom agreements or beliefs.

   Ask teachers to take five minutes each month for classroom discussion.

Involve supervisors in establishing beliefs
and rules.

Diane's time with these supervisors appeared to
them to have been profitable, focusing on solutions
rather than complaints and producing some specific
directions toward solutions. The consultant and the
group were congratulating themselves on their accom-
plishments, and they were eager to share their list with
the principal.

Judy had had a different kind of day. Besides her
daily duties as principal, she had been greeting 180
new kindergarten parents, supervising a videotaping
crew, and coordinating a schedule for a consultant
working in the building. Suddenly she was faced with
an exuberant team who had reinvented the lunchroom.
Was this what she needed?

She said to herself, "I knew I shouldn't have left
Diane alone with this group! I know I should have stayed
to offer a reality-based perspective. I should have told
Diane my picture of her job! She doesn't know anything about running a primary school."

Nonplussed, Judy drew upon old organized behaviors. In her frustration she made such statements as,
"We've tried that before and it didn't work; the students
won't eat their lunches if we do that; the parents will
complain; we don't have enough staff to supervise this
change."

Diane recognized that she may have offered ex-
cessively zealous leadership for change—in fact may
even have gone off the track altogether. She tried to

salvage the exchange and restitute herself with reassuring comments: "Sometimes a plan doesn't work the first time that works the second or third time; Deming says ninety-four percent of the problem is the system, only six percent is the people; Champlin says, 'We have to skin our own skunks'."

For some reason, these comments provided little comfort to a beleaguered principal suddenly foreseeing chaos in a previously stable area of the school. At about this time, the bell rang calling the supervisors to the first lunch. Saved by the bell! As they filed out, Diane collapsed in gales of laughter, asking Judy, "Is this the kind of principal you want to be? Is what you're doing getting you what you want?"

Judy rose to the challenge of self-evaluation, and Diane completed her own restitution by helping Judy figure out hers. They affirmed that it was okay to make a mistake, that perfection was not a human condition. They agreed it could have been worse if voices had been raised, the word "wrong" used, or the life-saving bell not rung.

Judy analyzed the old organized behavior she didn't like to see herself using and discovered that her motivation had been trying to stay in control and avoid upheaval. She did not want to repeat previous mistakes.

Examining those values, she concluded that they had served her well in the past, but that was not the kind of principal she wanted to be in this situation. Her restitution would be to meet again with the assistants to provide them a typed copy of their suggestions, to validate the importance of their contributions, and to plan how they could implement some of their ideas. She carried out her restitution a week later.

She opened this meeting by modeling self-evaluation. "After your meeting with Diane and me the other day," she told them, "Diane gave me some feedback. Once I finished laughing at myself, I realized I was not the kind of principal I wanted to be. I didn't want us to make the same mistakes over again, and that was important to me, but I don't like how I did it. So today I want to make a restitution and be more like the kind of principal I do want to be."

She talked to them about her beliefs. "I believe ninety-four percent of the problem is in the system; people in the system are the best people to fix the problem; we can learn from our mistakes; all people in the system have influence."

She described her view of herself, "I don't want to be a person who uses killer phrases. I laughed at myself when I recalled the killer phrases I used the other day—'It will never work, we tried that before, it's too late in the year to change.' My job is to support you in redesigning the system."

She discussed with them their ideas about redesigning the lunchroom procedure; she listened to them. Essentially what she heard was that, rather than formally dismissing each table, they wanted students to go outside freely after they finished eating. They thought this would reduce the noise problem.

Since these assistants were not working in the lunchroom when this procedure was tried earlier, she gave them some information about why it didn't work. There had been two main problems—students threw their food away in a big rush to go outside, and students ran helter-skelter from the lunchroom to the playground. Talking together about how to avoid these previous problems, they decided to talk to the students about the new procedure and try to identify common solutions.

They met with the students and asked them, "What do you want?" The students wanted to go out as soon as they finished eating rather than waiting for their table to be dismissed. They were told, "That's what we want too," sharing common ground. After telling these students about the two problems which had arisen before, they demonstrated "yes, if..." by saying, "Yes, you can go out when you're through eating, if you eat your food and walk—don't run—from the lunchroom to the playground."

After Judy, the assistants, and the students redesigned the system, the problem of noise did indeed improve. It was a win/win/win solution.

Students were excited with the new lunchroom procedures. They not only enjoyed going out to recess sooner, but they seemed pleased that they could succeed with the problems that caused failure in the past. The students were empowered—they discovered they could do something to get what they wanted, and they learned they could influence the system.

The assistants were also pleased with the new procedure. They reported that their job was easier and they were having more fun with the kids. Best of all, on the last day of school, one of the assistants asked Judy if they could be included in any discussions with staff about the lunchroom or playground procedures in the fall. Her interest confirmed for Judy that she had been the kind of principal she wanted to be. She had created the conditions for this assistant to feel empowered— she experienced having influence, and she believed she could fix the system.

Judy was strengthened, learning to laugh at her mistake, to accept feedback, to use best knowledge, and to try again to solve a problem and increase involvement. It took courage to evaluate herself in the presence of staff. It was a risk to try again a procedure which had already failed. But it surely paid off. Would she do it again? Yes. Judy believes in the power of self-evaluation to restore her own balance and to renew the system she leads.

QUALITY LEADERSHIP

We have said before that every person is a unique individual control system. We have emphasized the importance therefore of reducing coercion and increasing collegiality so that individuals are free to experience their own homeorhesis while forming and contributing to a community of quality. But this "community-making," as Scott Peck says, "requires time as well as effort and sacrifice." To reach true community, individuals decide to let themselves be vulnerable, giving up their attempts to control outcomes.

If a control system is meant to be in control, then renewal will contain frustration, especially for leaders, whose job it is to foster the non-coercive, risk-taking, ever-changing environment for continuous celebration of the evolution toward quality.

So how do you maintain balance and sustain energy for this very exciting, but very difficult job? We have identified three characteristic attributes of quality leaders: (1) they learn to relish cognitive complexity, (2) they are proactive, and (3) they are brave.

The paradigm shift of getting started, the deepening opportunity for involvement during moving forward, the skills for getting unstuck, the techniques for aligning practices—all the learning of the early stages of change are part of your permanent equipment, and all with use develop an increasing strength and facility through continuing renewal.

To hone them ever more sharply seems to generate the personal strengths which characterize leaders who continuously celebrate renewal for themselves and in their organizations. These are the strengths that give meaning to the skills we try to teach, that enable us to believe that out of disorder and frustration comes new order and growth toward quality.

COGNITIVE COMPLEXITY

Develop the ability to deal with cognitive complexity. Learn new information about shifting paradigms, systems theory, and control theory, each of which depends upon right-brain thinking. The right brain loves paradox and complexity; the right brain thrives on questions which have no immediately apparent answers.

The questions of concern to those who lead large organizations are right-brain questions:

1. What are the sources of order?

2. How do you create organizational coherence, where activities correspond to purpose?

3. How do you create structures that move with change, that are flexible and adaptive,

even boundaryless, that enable rather than constrain?

4. How do you simplify things without losing both control and differentiation?

5. How do you reconcile personal needs for freedom and autonomy with organizational needs for prediction and control?

Margaret Wheatley, Leadership and the New Science.

These are right-brain questions: paradoxical, complex, without simple, obvious answers. Addressing them requires cognitive complexity.

Like us, you probably were educated in a system that prized left-brain, linear thinking, which focused on the right or wrong answers. The two of us found that studying control theory and systems thinking shifted our mental models to a totally different way of learning. In college, studying a set of ideas and making it our own had been relatively simple. In our new course of study, we learned to relish cognitive complexity.

We needed to take in information from a variety of sources over a period of time. Then we needed to leave it alone for a while as our brain sifted, ordered, and created new wholes of understanding our experience. Sometimes this process created not just wholes, but holes in our understanding, which spurred anew the search for knowledge. Do not be afraid of this kind of learning. Be patient and inviting with yourself. Honor the need for time and interim confusion.

We learned to perceive new input neutrally, not prejudging but seeking to understand. Control theory predicts how difficult this can be, because your filters are how you organize your perceptions; they help you be in control of what is coming in from the world. You can learn to change your perceptions, but a shift in the higher levels results in all the lower-level perceptions being re-aligned. When this occurs, it is at best disconcerting and may be quite chaotic. Developing a tolerance, or better, a taste for this kind of chaos means trusting the process.

> When things are most chaotic, when everything appears to be destroyed, that is when the greatest change occurs and things then begin to calm down.
>
> *Jennifer James*

Cognitive complexity is an acquired taste for most people. Not only is traditional moral and academic training rather left-brained, but English does not have the kind of vocabulary that lends itself to this sort of thinking. While writing this book, we searched for a word to describe the capacity to see everything from more than one angle. We found no adequate English description.

The Chinese symbol, the radical, embodies this concept. For example, the symbol for freedom carries within it the visual construct of bondage. A more familiar example is the radical for crisis, which incorporates both opportunity and danger. Hindi has these concepts, and so do Japanese and the North American Indian languages. European languages lack this richness of perspective, so cognitive complexity is more difficult for those whose first language is English.

The complexity we recognize as essential for continuing renewal does not mean merely complexity of detail, but rather complexity of perspective. Learn to stand and view a phenomenon from many angles. Learn to look at the positive side of a negative and the negative side of a positive. Learn to play the devil's advocate to pull up consideration of any opposite.

A complex thinker understands the importance of context in assessing a situation. A complex thinker learns to validate the intent of what appears to be misbehavior by seeking the useful purpose of the behavior. A complex thinker understands that each individual creates reality by choosing perceptions on the dark side or the bright.

Every brilliant invention carries within it the potential for abuse. The complex thinker knows that this is not a black/white, right/wrong world. With cognitive complexity, you will become increasingly flexible of mind and heart and thereby increase your capacity for control—another paradox.

PROACTION

Another source of control is proaction, the opposite of reaction. Stimulus-response psychology says behavior is a response to what others do. Control theory psychology says behavior is always created from an internal referent, that you are always trying to self-actualize to some ideal created internally.

In a crisis, rather than reacting to criticism or coercion from others, understand that the only person under control is yourself, and that is who is motivated to behave. Ask, "Who do I want to be in this difficult situation? How can I stay my course and still be the person I want to be despite attempts of others to make me reactive, to control me emotionally?"

Sometimes you will be criticized by others. When that happens, it is important to recognize that the person criticizing is trying to pull you to the feeling level. If you let the critics succeed in that, you'll be off balance. Keep yourself balanced by thinking, "Isn't it interesting how this person is trying to control me. Will I let it work?"

Approach it this way, and you bring yourself from feeling to thinking and get some balance. Ask the person what he or she wants. This gives you an action to do and keeps you in control of yourself. People, when they criticize, are telling you what they don't want. Try saying to them, "You're telling me what you don't like. Tell me how you would like to see this solved." Stick up for yourself. If you don't agree with what the person has said, say, "I understand that's your opinion. I see it a little differently."

Try to avoid becoming defensive or criticizing others. When you are criticized, reply, "This is not how to get what you want from me." You might also say, "This conversation is not helping. I don't want to fight with you." If a situation becomes inflammatory, defuse it by calmly leaving and saying, "This is not how I want to be talking about this. I'd like to talk to you when things are calmed down. I want to work this out later."

As we did in the above example of planning in advance how to answer criticism without losing balance, try to foresee problems, to avoid them if possible, and to prepare solutions before they are needed. This solution focus is characteristic of quality leadership, and so is a preference for long-term fundamental solutions which remove problems, not people, from the system.

For example, a behavior problem might be solved by sending the disrupting student to the principal for discipline. The problem would then be removed from the classroom: the teacher could teach and the remaining students could learn. In the long run, however, the disrupting student doesn't learn more effective behaviors and probably doesn't even meet the need underlying the less effective behavior. Worse, the momentum for change is eroded as the short-term solution takes pressure off the system. Worst of all, you have compromised the value you hold for inclusiveness.

Long-term solutions will produce more fundamental change in the system without violating a belief, so that this student and the others *all* could get their needs met. Possibilities are limited only by energy and commitment and creativity:

> Implement new multisensory ways for the student to learn with reduced frustration.

> Train parent volunteers in the techniques of reality therapy so that they can work individually with difficult students in the classroom.

> Reset district priorities to make funds available for teacher assistants who can facilitate inclusion.

Some of these are very ambitious, to be sure. Aren't they exciting to contemplate! You may rightfully say they are too difficult, too expensive, too time-consuming, too idealistic. That may well be true and often is. But try always to be mindful of the need to search for and sometimes try for long-term solutions compatible with all your values. In a quality organization, short-term solutions are used for short-term problems. For long-term problems, proactive leaders apply such solutions only to buy safety, time, or support for a solution which will strengthen the system.

Being proactive also can sometimes be very simple. For example, a teacher, beginning to think about the ten years remaining before her retirement, asked, "How do I want to be remembered by people at the end of my career?" Realizing that she wanted to be remembered as caring and growing, she began to attend workshops to help herself create a more democratic classroom. Though change was a challenge, she became the person she envisioned. She has not retired yet and has reset her ideal higher several times.

By projecting into the future and calling up the ideal situation you want to happen, you are creating the design you want to find in the world. The rest of the process is simply tracking back from the ideal, developing the small steps necessary to arrive at the desired destination.

A proactive leader spends little time regretting past mistakes but rather gleans new learnings for next time. Anticipate difficulties. Recognize that you are part of the change process, and self-evaluate when you make a mistake. Allow others the same privilege. Address the system rather than targeting individuals.

COURAGE

Demonstrate courage. Stephen Covey talks about the importance of balancing courage and consideration. From our experience, we believe most leaders can ascertain whether they are too strong in courage, which puts them in a win/lose position, or too strong in consideration, which puts them in a lose/win position, accommodating too often to the requests of staff.

You will need a good measure of courage for the challenges you will face in system change. Though you seldom will face physical danger, you may risk loss of face or position or security. You can gain courage from the following:

Having strong personal convictions.

Having had your opinion validated as a child, being listened to by someone significant in the present.

Believing in the intrinsic humanity and goodness in people.

Understanding that to lose a battle may mean to win a war or that to win a battle may mean to lose a war.

Operating from the level of personal awareness where who you will be is more important than what you will lose or what you will gain or who will like you.

It is an awesome moment when someone stands on principle, particularly in the face of authority or against popular opinion or at high personal risk. The group always knows when this is happening. Such courage is seldom foolhardy but carefully considered. This stance comes from the very being of a person to be reckoned with. This person has risen to be counted, overcoming personal fear and in the face of potential danger—always on a matter of principle!

The person is operating in control-theory terms from the system of values, which prescribes how people ought to treat each other in the world. When you make a decision at this level, it has ramifications for your principles and your practices. The room is always awed and silent when such courage is shown.

In our work in the quality school movement, we have witnessed courage in the following:

An assistant superintendent confronting a superintendent who has scuttled a delicate staff/management negotiation by coercion.

A participant in a district training standing up for the trainers who are being criticized in the absence of representation.

An administrator taking responsibility for a financial overrun rather than blaming subordinates.

A principal standing behind a staff person who has raised the ire of parents.

In each of these cases the group, be it a school staff or a district staff, recognized the personal courage needed by the individual to make a stand. Even though they did not necessarily agree with the point being made, the group honored the individual's commitment to the belief, recognizing that it was at personal risk and took considered courage. By operating on principle, this person spoke to the heart of all, regardless of others' investments in the issue. This is not the courage of the saber-rattler or the zealot.

Not all courage is overt. Courage to stay a course, to maintain quiet alignment in the face of pressure to abandon reform, also draws respect. Again it must be stressed, respect is not asking for blind adherence. It is asking for the thoughtful, considered taking of a position which is tied to a higher value. This tie to the value is most often verbally stated by the person making a stand.

Lost opportunities for courage also abound:

Covert racism is not confronted.

An effective consultant who questions alignment of expectations and practices is not rehired.

A group says nothing as one of its members verbally abuses a coordinator.

A political appointment is made at the expense of the best candidate.

A toxic teacher remains in the classroom.

The scenarios are numerous. They are lost opportunities for a group to grow through the individual's courage. People will not follow on a new course with a leader who is without courage. But the road to change is rocky, and even the most personally courageous leader is well advised to seek support.

School Example:

A Principal Has Courage

What follows shows principal Tom Kennedy using courage to act as a catalyst for self-renewal in his school. He had concluded that he was not being the principal he wanted to be and found the courage to address it. This is the text of the speech he wrote and delivered.

> As we start, just let me say that my delivery during the next few minutes may be somewhat awkward and sometimes disjointed. Whenever I feel strongly about something I often get in a random mode, so please bear with me.... The subject I feel so strongly about is "where we have been, where we are, and where we are going!"
>
> I'm disappointed and upset with myself with regard to the "where we are" and "where we are going." I have enabled some of us, with regard to change, to remain where we were when we first met together in August of 1990. I have not facilitated or created a need for change, and so with some of us a high per cent of classroom practices remain in a soft, warm comfort zone. What I have enabled is not fair! Not fair to you, not fair to your colleagues, not fair to your students, not fair to the parents of your students, and not fair to the school district.
>
> The district has done and continues to do its part...It has provided opportunities for high quality inservices, high quality classes and training, and high quality conferences. For the most part, they

are changing the way they do business to better meet the needs of the students and employees.

It is inappropriate for me to stand in the way, by means of my enabling, of quality learning for our students. It's inappropriate for me to not work to help extinguish some of the current classroom practices that don't promote quality learning for our students! The old adage, "You're either part of the solution or you're part of the problem," well...I've been part of the problem.

My goal is to discontinue being part of the problem and become part of the solution. My project, for next year and years to come, is to ask tough questions and continue asking the tough questions until we are serving the highest quality educational services to our customers that we are capable of! These questions may, at times, seem confrontational, they may be very uncomfortable...but you will need to realize that they will be directed at the professional, not the personal. The first question is: "Are you doing what is good for the learner? Are you offering every learner an opportunity for quality learning? And are you working hard to ensure that every learner grasps the opportunity?"

The asking of the tough questions will not be easy for me and many times, probably, not go real smoothly...but I am committed to this change in my behavior. The tough questions are going to be self-evaluative questions, and they may hurt and cause anxious times as you self-examine. I know, I've been going through this process. My expectation for you is that you will make responsible decisions based on your examination and take appropriate action!

You may very well be sitting there thinking..."Who the hell does he think he is, invading my comfort zone?" Well the questions will probably invade your comfort zone often! Maybe you have heard of the popular upper-grade book *13 Ways to Sink the Substitute*. Well, after 21 years in the classroom and working under seven different principals, I know there are at least 100 ways to sink the principal—and I welcome that! I hope you get so fed up with my questions and prying that you vow to butt heads with me and to prove that what is happening in your classroom is supported by current research, action research, authentic assessment, end products from kids, and kids engaged in the process for quality learning. If you do nail my ears to the wall with that evidence, then we will have done our job, because you will be doing what is best for kids.

At that time, we will both be able to proudly say that we are part of the solution. On the other hand, if the questions are going to be too painful—and I can appreciate that—I then invite you, as I do yearly, to seek a new environment, one that meets your needs. Change is good, and we are going to diligently work on change!

To the individuals that are actively self-evaluating, making responsible professional decisions, and then taking action: you have a responsibility. You have the responsibility to share, coach, give feedback, model, etc. We cannot produce quality results if we isolate ourselves...We ALL have responsibilities to ALL our students and parents,

not just our classroom! If the thought..."Is he talking to me?" or "Is he talking about me?" is going
through your head, then you have begun the self-
evaluative process. Continue that process! Ask for
honest feedback from colleagues!!

The Building Leadership Team is going to facilitate the rest of the afternoon...I hope you will actively and honestly participate and come to a
consensus with regard to a document that will
serve as a guide for our continued journey! Good
afternoon, I'll see you tommorrow!

Continuous
Celebration

An organization advanced in creating the conditions for quality will be able to celebrate even its problems. Not long ago, for example, staff at Sheridan Hills were frustrated by the number of visitors who were coming to their school for visits. They were beginning to feel like they were performing in a fish bowl. They did not want so many people in the school. They wanted to focus on the learning process with their students. It was not that they disliked helping others, but they identified a need for freedom to experiment without being observed.

They knew they had to do something different, so they raised this question at a staff meeting, where they agreed to a moratorium on visits until the next fall, so they would have time to make a better plan. They also began to design back to the solution they wanted.

They would be told in advance when visitors were expected. Teachers would reserve the right to decide whether visitors could visit their classrooms. Perhaps it would be possible to hire a floating substitute so teachers would be free to talk with visitors.

As they planned their solution and recognized how many options they had, staff no longer felt the frustration which had arisen from lack of freedom, and their power need was met by planning to be able to accept recognition and make a contribution.

Is this the kind of problem you would like to be having—too much of a good thing? Is this the way you would like to be solving your problems? The journey to quality is quite exciting, and continuing renewal sustains the excitement.

A quality school celebrates its growth through continuing renewal, and this celebration flows outward to district and community and inward to students. In this chapter, we provide three final examples of creating the conditions for quality: continuing renewal in a district and in a community, and a self-renewing student who represents the ideals of a Quality School.

DISTRICT RENEWAL

Continuing renewal at the district level is an aspect of the process that few districts work on intentionally. Leaders in cross-functional teams are always involved in creating the vision and the exit outcomes, and this association also deserves to be continued for evaluating whether outcomes are realistic and whether they are being achieved.

One district which has chosen to institutionalize a process of continual evaluation of expectations is the staff of the Evergreen School District in Vancouver, Washington. They have worked with Dr. John Champlin to monitor their alignment. They have a dinner meeting every three months with over 100 participants from a staff of 1700. They self-evaluate their personal practices and evaluate where their work units are in the change process.

Each session has a training component, a self-evaluation component, and a social component. Topics openly discussed in the large group are such as "Are we reducing coercion?" and "Are we willing to receive feedback?" The superintendent and deputy superintendent attend and actively participate in these sessions.

In addition, a core team of eight people, representing all program areas, meet with their Quality School consultant monthly to be sure they are using control theory in their interactions. The Responsible Decision Making summary of control-theory skills guides Evergreen's process of continuing alignment. We offer it here to guide your continuing renewal through self-evaluation.

Figure 24. **Responsible Decision Making**

Responsible decision making means you can implement the following strategies and self-evaluate your practice of them.

Identify the psychological needs.

Identify the components of behavior.

Recognize when you experience a failure mode or a success mode.

Ask the four reality therapy questions:

What do you want?

What are you doing?

Is it working?

Do you want to make a new plan?

Identify how you are using words (10%), tone (35%), and nonverbal communication (55%).

Complain efficiently and redirect complainers by asking "How would you like it to be?" or "What do you see as a solution?"

Do a role clarification in the form of *My Job is....*

Use the Success Connection for problem-solving.

Use *Does it Really Matter?* and "Yes, if..." management.

Change your pictures by going from an unattainable want to find the need and create a new picture.

Reinvent yourself by using thinking to get new action to change feelings, following Barnes Boffey's model in *Reinventing Yourself* (Chapel Hill, NC: New View, 1993).

Use the Take Control Chart to self-assess.

Identify three filters for taking in information:

(a) Sensory: "What I see, hear, etc."

(b) Knowledge: "What I add from my experience, etc." (best knowledge)

(c) Value: "What I value based on my quality world pictures."

Self-evaluate starting with "What I appreciate about myself..."and by asking, "Could I have done worse?"

We believe this list pretty well summarizes what we have tried to teach. If you have mastered all these skills, then you will understand why we think continuing renewal is a continuous celebration.

COMMUNITY RENEWAL

There is a district in North Carolina which has worked together to create for the community a Quality School picture that reflects the values of that community. This district is Fuquay-Varina. Kay Currin, one of the parents of this community, is serving on the international Quality School Consortium Board, and she summarized their work in *Schools Magazine* in Spring, 1994.

In the winter of 1992, a handful of parents, businessmen, and educators came together to discuss what we could do as a community in Fuquay-Varina to improve our schools. We are part of a very large school district in Wake County.

We started to meet as a group to consider what impact we could have on the education of our children. Most of us agreed that it was not just doing the same things better, but that we would need to begin to conceptualize and move toward a new system. Our Chamber of Commerce president, Bob Baker, supported what we call the Fuquay-Varina Area Education Foundation. He was committed to our mission and volunteered for the position of president.

We invited Dr. Willard Daggett, the Director of the International Center for Leadership in Education, to be our Chamber of Commerce speaker in April, 1992. Dr. Daggett spoke with business leaders, area teachers, parents, and the community about the educational crisis we face as a nation. Most importantly, he gave us a management process for change that has been our guiding light.

The first step in the process was to create an awareness of the need for change. Today, we need to be aware that the skills, knowledge, and behavior needed for employment outweigh those needed for higher education. Our schools primarily focus on preparing young people for college. This has prevented us from achieving world-class standards.

We are currently educating our community. We have sponsored staff-development workshops for our teachers and administrators. We sent thirty people to hear Dr. William Glasser, author of *The Quality School*, speak in Raleigh last December and invited him to speak at our third Chamber of Commerce banquet.

Fortunately, we were able to bring Dr. Al Mamary, former superintendent of Johnson City Schools in New York, to be our Chamber speaker last year. He spent one day with our faculty discussing how his belief that all children can learn helped his own staff move toward an inclusive system. Children in Johnson City Schools believed they could learn because no one told them they couldn't.

Our next event is a community forum to discuss what it will take to create the schools to carry our children into the 21st century. We want to involve everyone in this process—the community, civic groups, churches, parents, business, students, and families. Dr. Daggett closed his talk with these words: "Use the love you have for your own children to motivate you to do what we need to do. Love your children more than you love your schools."

I would encourage anyone interested in systemic change to be determined in their efforts. Get key people to learn and attend seminars so that you will share a common belief about students and their learning. As one superintendent said, "we know what to do and how to do it. Love your children enough that you will become an advocate for all of our children."

CONCLUSION

We have attempted in this book to share some of our experiences on the road to quality. We focus on the wisdom of control theory. Control-theory thinking provides an analytical model with the depth necessary for developing cognitive complexity. We have tried to show you how control theory can help you create conditions for quality. Control theory offers a structure for your thinking.

This structure says you are internally motivated. You create what you want in your head and then find in the world a perception that matches what you want. Your control system is a pull system, not a push system. Your vision pulls your behavior. William Powers entitled his book *Behavior: The Control of Perception* (Chicago: Aldine de Gruyter, 1973), emphasizing that behavior is the attempt to achieve what is already internally visualized.

Ask people to create their personal visions, then to create shared visions for which they can seek together. The process of creating the vision lends energy to the task of actualizing it. This process is more important than the vision itself, because a control system is a pull system, not a push system. Quality leadership is proactive, and therefore it is always searching with the group to discover a common goal.

Use control theory to analyze what you experience. Whenever there is a disturbance, view it as a signal that some internal goal has shifted. Rather than focusing on the disruption, try to ascertain what goal has changed. Even deviant behavior can be found purposeful if you view it as created to meet a need.

We have offered you the Take Control Chart as a tool for identifying internal purposes. When you follow this process and share the information, individuals can align their goals with group purpose.

Control theory shows interrelationships instead of linear causal interactions. Whatever one is doing at any given moment is meeting a goal created by that person. All behavior is an attempt to meet some need, and all behavior is purposeful. To view an individual's behavior as directed outwardly against someone else is not as fruitful as understanding that the behavior is created to meet an internal goal, and that goal can be intentionally modified.

Learn to use the questions of reality therapy to assist individuals in distress, including yourself, self-evaluate chosen goals and collapse perceived conflict among needs. You never need to be critical of others if you recognize internal motivation. You will be able to understand, not to judge, the process of change.

Understanding gives courage, the courage that comes from a higher purpose. Your purpose becomes twofold— maximizing degrees of freedom for individuals, and helping create new goals which meet many people's needs and which therefore have much energy.

Control theory helps us to operate as the individual self-regulating systems we are. We had a lot of learning to undo, because we grew up in a behaviorist system, so that we first tended to look externally rather than internally. We hope this book will help you to focus first internally, and to look always for the sense rather than the nonsense in a situation. Remember, create what you want from life. Pull it from the world and read your own deviations as signposts for future directions to take. When in doubt, return yourself to the kind of person you want to be.

Renewal is not the end of the process. Renewal is the process. Renewal is taking place as you read this page; renewal is taking place even if you throw this book across the room. What is it you are reaching for? Who are you becoming at this moment?

Someone in a workshop this year said to Diane, "Five years from now you'll be espousing another theory. You'll have abandoned what you're talking about now and be on a new bandwagon." She answered, "I hope so! I hope I am looking at everything I now understand with new eyes one level up on the spiral of understanding."

APPENDIX

A. Richfield Public Schools
Mission Statement

The mission of the Richfield Public Schools is to prepare all students for a changing world by developing individual abilities and talents within a climate of mutual respect and trust.

Beliefs that drive the Teaching/Learning Process in the Richfield Public Schools:

We believe in

Growth through change

Development of all students' gifts, talents and creativity

Mutual respect and trust

Family and community involvement

The significance of cultural diversity and global awareness

High expectations

Quality

Prevention

Time to learn

Teaching to the correct level of difficulty

Inclusiveness

Focus on outcomes

Optimism

Success

Cooperation

Power of praise and affirmation

Decisions based upon best knowledge

Reasonable risk

The power of vision

Exit Outcomes

Acquire, integrate, and be able to use knowledge from the disciplines at the levels of:

Recall

Comprehension

Application

Analysis

Synthesis

Evaluation

Acquire and be able to use the process skills of:

> Group dynamics
>
> Problem solving
>
> Communication
>
> Conflict resolution
>
> Decision making
>
> Feel competent and valued
>
> Show concern and respect for others
>
> Be self-directed and lifelong learners

Beliefs can change over time due to experience and new information. Therefore, these belief statements will be reviewed periodically.

Values

> Achievement of Desired Outcomes
>
> Collaboration/Cooperation
>
> Commitment
>
> Creativity
>
> Courage
>
> Dignity/Respect
>
> Diversity
>
> Empathy and Openness in Relationships
>
> Integrity
>
> Responsible Behavior
>
> Trust
>
> Uniqueness in Learners
>
> Validated Knowledge

Ethics
We will:

Act honestly and openly in dealing with all clients and colleagues

Act purposefully to create conditions for success and creativity

Increase benefits and eliminate harm to clients

Live beliefs and value knowledge

Live within parameters of agreements/ contracts

Respect confidentiality

Respond to behaviors that are not aligned

Seek out and apply best knowledge

B. Sheridan Hills Classroom Agreements

Kindergarten
Room 120 Class Agreement
1. We want our class to be the best that we can be.
2. We want to be friends and be nice to each other.
3. We want to work hard.
4. We want to take care of our room and of Sheridan Hills.

Grade 1

A Real, Nice, Wonderful Family of Friends

We agree that:

> Friends share and care
>
> They use nice talk and good manners
>
> They care about each other,
>
> They help each other and share with each other.
>
> Friends do their best
>
> They do quality work
>
> They try when it's hard and keep trying,
>
> They share their best with others.
>
> Friends take care of the environment
>
> They take care of the classroom and everything in it,
>
> They take care of all the earth.

Written by the first grade students in room 105
Sheridan Hills School
1994-1995

Amanda
Britta
MarMar
BriANS.
Cecilia
ZAcK
chris Cory Devon
Ms. Bell
Greg Nataliya Jessica
Kyle Nicole
Nicole
Peter Luke
JaMte

Grade 2

Dear Families,

Our class has been spending a lot of time these past few days discussing how we want things in our classroom to be this year. In keeping with the Sheridan Hills belief that we respect ourselves, each other, our work, and our environment, we have reached an agreement as a class.

We have agreed that in our classroom we will:

1. respect and be nice to each other.

2. stay safe by being careful and keeping hands and feet to ourselves.

3. listen to each other.

4. take care of our classroom and the things in it.

5. share and include each other.

6. do our best.

Everyone in the room will be expected to live up to this agreement. We will work together to make our classroom a satisfying, safe place for us all. Together we are the best we can be!

Sincerely,

The Students and Teachers of A-15

Grade 3

Belief Statement:

At Sheridan Hills we respect ourselves, others, our work and our environment.

Together we are the best we can be.

Classroom Agreement:

Be responsible for our work.

Be respectful to ourselves and others.

Have the power to learn and keep ourselves in control.

Be positive and have fun.

Take risks, mistakes are OK.

We want school to be challenging.

C. Concerns-Based Adoption Model (CBAM) and *Creating the Conditions*

	Level	Concern	Section and Chapter
Internalize and Impact	6	Refocusing	Continuing Renewal
	5	Collaboration	Aligning Practices: Problem-Solving
	4	Consequences	Getting Unstuck: Conflict Resolution
Task	3	Management	Moving Forward: Reality Therapy
Self	2	Personal	Getting Started: Control Theory
	1	Information	Getting Started: Quality School Concept
Introduction	0	Awareness	

REFERENCES

Anderson, Judith A. *Microcomputer Exposure Related to Elementary Teacher Concerns About the Educational Use of Computers.* Thesis, 1985.

Aronstein, Laurence W., Marcia Marlow, & Randan Desilets. "Detours on the Road to Site-Based Management." *Educational Leadership,* April 1990.

Barth, Roland. "A Personal Vision of a Good School," *Phi Delta Kappan,* March 1990.

Boffey, Barnes. *Reinventing Yourself.* Chapel Hill: New View Publications, 1993.

Chambers, Arthur J. *Success Connection Questions.* Johnson City Central School, December 1991.

Cohen, Herb. *You Can Negotiate Anything.* New York: Bantam Books, 1980.

Covey, Stephen R. *Principle-Centered Leadership.* New York: Summit Books, 1991.

Covey, Stephen R. *The 7 Habits of Highly Effective People.* New York: Simon & Schuster Inc., 1989.

Currin, Kay. "The Fuquay-Varina Area Education Foundation." *Schools,* Spring 1994, pp. 10-11.

Deming, W. Edwards. *The New Economics for Industry, Government, Education.* Cambridge: Massachusetts Institute of Technology, 1993.

Gardner, John. *On Leadership.* New York: Free Press, 1989.

Gardner, John. *The Tasks of Leadership.* Washington, D.C.: Leadership Studies Program, 1986.

Glasser, William. *Diagram of the Brain as a Control System.* Canoga Park: Institute for Control Theory, Reality Therapy, & Quality Management 1986.

Glasser, William. *The Quality School.* New York: Harper & Row, 1990.

Glasser, William. *The Quality School Teacher.* New York: HarperCollins, 1993.

Glasser, William. *Schools Without Failure.* New York: Harper & Row, 1969.

Glickman, Carl D. *Renewing America's Schools: A Guide for School-Based Education.* San Francisco: Jossey-Bass Publishers, 1993.

Good, E. Perry. *Helping Kids Help Themselves.* Chapel Hill: New View Publications, 1992.

Good, E. Perry. *In Pursuit of Happiness.* Chapel Hill: New View Publications, 1987.

Good, E. Perry. *It's OK to Be the Boss.* Chapel Hill: New View Publications, 1990.

Gossen, Diane. *Control Theory in Action.* Saskatoon, Saskatchewan: Chelsom Consultants, 1987.

Gossen, Diane. *My Child Is a Pleasure to Live With.* Saskatoon, Saskatchewan: Chelsom Consultants, 1987,

Gossen, Diane. *Restitution: Restructuring School Discipline.* Chapel Hill: New View Publications, 1992.

Green, Hannah. *I Never Promised You a Rose Garden.* New York: Holt, Reinhardt & Winston, 1957.

Hord, Shirley, William Rutherford, Leslie Hulung-Austin, & Gene Hall. *Taking Charge of Change.* Alexandria, VA: Association for Supervision and Curriculum Development, 1987.

Kohn, Alfie. *Punished by Rewards*. New York: Houghton-Mifflin, 1993.

Mamary, Al. "A Framework for Quality Learning." Unpublished article.

Mapes, James J. "Foresight First," *Sky,* September 1991.

McDowell, Floyd. "Developmentally Appropriate Primary Phase Education and School Improvement." *Quality Outcomes-Driven Education,* December 1993 (Volume 3, Number 2),

Miller, J. G. *Living Systems,* New York: McGraw-Hill, 1978.

Mintz, Jeffrey. *Workplace Needs Survey* (with computer software). Institute for Management Development, Inc., 1992.

Neave, Henry R. *The Deming Dimension*. Knoxville, TN: SPC Press, Inc., 1990.

Peck, M. Scott. *The Different Drum: Community Making and Peace*. New York: Touchstone, 1988.

Perdue, Mona and Mariwyn Tinsley. *The Journey to Quality*. Chapel Hill: New View Publications, 1992.

Robert Pirsig. *Lila: An Inquiry into Morals*. New York: Bantam, 1992.

Powers, William. *Behavior: The Control of Perception*. Chicago: Aldine de Gruyter, 1973.

Powers, William. "Degrees of Freedom in Social Interactions." in *Living Control Systems: Selected Papers of William T. Powers*. Gravel Switch, KY: The Control Systems Group, 1989.

Senge, Peter. *The Fifth Discipline*. New York: Doubleday, 1990.

Tannen, Deborah. *You Just Don't Understand*. New York: Ballantine Books, 1990.

Wheatley, Margaret. *Leadership and the New Science: Learning About Organization from an Orderly Universe*. San Francisco: Berrett-Koehler Publishers Inc., 1992.

Wilson, James Q. *The Moral Sense*. New York: Macmillan, Inc., 1993.

INDEX OF FIGURES

About the Authors

Diane Gossen is an educator and management consultant from Saskatoon, Saskatchewan. A Senior Faculty member of the Institute for Control Theory, Reality Therapy and Quality Management, she has taught reality therapy and control theory internationally for twenty years.

Diane has also trained school districts throughout the United States and Canada in Quality School ideas, and has worked for several years with the Saskatchewan Department of Justice and the Saskatchewan Alcohol and Drug Abuse Foundation.

She is the author of *Control Theory in Action* (1989), *Restitution: Restructuring School Discipline* (1992), and *The Restitution: Restructuring School Discipline Facilitator's Guide* (1994). In addition, she is featured in the Video Journal of Education in the segment "Dealing with Disruptive and Unmotivated Students."

Judy Anderson is an elementary principal from Minnesota. Her school, Sheridan Hills, has joined the Quality School Consortium and is implementing Dr. William Glasser's Quality School ideas. Judy is presently the Chair of the Board of Directors for the Quality School Consortium, and is also a faculty member for the Institute for Control Theory, Reality Therapy, and Quality Management.

Both Diane and Judy are featured in New View Multimedia's Restitution Staff Development Training Program videos.

Paid for from:
ATOD Prevention Program Funds
Eau Claire Area School District
500 Main Street
Eau Claire, WI 54701